Teacher's 2B Guide

Apple Pie

Delta's Beginning ESL Program

Sadae Iwataki, Editor

Jean Owensby
Constance Turner

REVISED EDITION

ISBN 0–937354–63–5

Delta Systems Co., Inc.
1400 Miller Parkway
McHenry, IL 60050 U.S.A.

Apple Pie 2B
Table of Contents

To the Teacher

Thank you for choosing Delta's **Apple Pie** as your ESL textbook. This series brings to you a comprehensive, carefully structured, realistically paced curriculum for the "beginning low" and "beginning high" levels, as defined by California's English as a Second Language Model Standards for Adult Education Programs, in four books: student books 1A and 1B for beginning low ESL and student books 2A and 2B for beginning high ESL. It is appropriate for adult and young adult learners in the United States and abroad. Its content and structure were developed over many years of use in the adult ESL programs of the Los Angeles Unified School District.

The following is a brief overview of the lesson structure of **Apple Pie**, and general directions for using the teaching notes in this guide.

Something New: Every lesson begins with this oral introduction of new material through use of visuals to accompany a listening comprehension selection. The target vocabulary and structures are introduced without the textbook through a series of steps: listen only, comprehension check, listen and repeat, listen and respond.

Let's Talk: This is a dialogue that incorporates the new language in the meaningful context of a dialogue set in a real–life situation. Students first master the dialogue orally with the help of a dialogue visual, then practice it with and without the teacher's help, and finally practice it with a partner and /or say it aloud from memory.

Practice, Interaction, Practice Activity: These are sections that expand on the language presented in the previous sections by using it again in mini–dialogues for pair practice, situations for role plays, group activities, and mixers. The practice sections move from more controlled oral work to more open–ended or personalized oral practice.

Reading: Reading passages are related to the lesson topic, using similar structures and vocabulary to present new information. They are followed by discussion questions, which generally end with a reference to students' own thoughts or experiences.

Writing: The writing sections provide review and reinforcement while giving students a chance to practice spelling and punctuation. In books 2A and 2B, some lessons have sections called ***More Writing***, which provide prompts for controlled or original writing of sentences and short paragraphs.

After the core lesson, it is important to continue using the new language by including the ***Review*** and ***Activity Pages*** in subsequent class sessions. This way students have many opportunities to internalize new structures and functions and use them in their everyday interactions in English. The *Activity Pages* may include focused listening exercises, "information gap" activities, games, mixers, reading and discussion of true stories, and other tasks that integrate the language skills in a variety of relevant, interesting activities which provide student–student interaction and skill–building opportunities.

After each of the eight units of three related lessons, there is an ***Evaluation***, with Listening Comprehension, Reading, and Writing sections. This regular evaluation is meant to be done individually and then corrected to give students an indication of their progress and teachers an indication of the current needs of the class.

An essential element in the pedagogy of **Apple Pie** is the use of the hand–held visuals available for each book. These contain the illustrations for the *Something New* and *Let's Talk* sections of the lessons, and are used to teach new vocabulary, structures, and functions with aural and visual cues for understanding. On the back of each visual are the phrases, sentences, or dialogue to be presented, to that the new language can be introduced as students listen without looking at the textbook.

The *Let's Talk* and *Reading* sections, focused listening sections of the *Activity Pages*, and Listening Comprehension sections of the *Evaluations* also appear on the **Apple Pie Cassette** available to accompany each book. Instructions are given in this teacher's guide for presenting those sections by using the cassette to provide opportunities for students to develop better listening skills by hearing different voices, by hearing new material before they read it, and by doing listening exercises that require them to glean information to carry out a task.

Guide to symbols used in the teacher's guide:

 The "closed book" symbol is a reminder that this is an oral section of the presentation, during which students are not yet looking at their books.

 This symbol means "now open your books" and indicates that students are about to see in print the items that they have been practicing orally.

 This group symbol indicates that students will be moving around the room in an interaction that requires them to speak to several students, or that they will be participating in a group activity.

 A cassette symbol in the heading means that a section is recorded on the tape, allowing an alternative presentation of the section by having students listen to a dialogue, listen while reading a passage, or listen and pick out specific information in a focused listening exercise.

At the beginning of each lesson in the teacher's guide, you will find Communication Objectives for the lesson, new structures that appear in the lesson, and a list of the visuals and other instructional aids needed for presenting the lesson to your class.

Good luck and success to you all. We hope that the **Apple Pie** program will serve you well, and that your students will find learning English our way to be effective, confidence–building and fun!

Lifestyles

Communication Objectives:
Discuss activities at senior centers
Ask and answer questions about habitual activities
Give instructions about everyday safety

New Structures:
Simple present
Frequency adverbs: *always, usually, sometimes, rarely, seldom, never*
Questions with *how often* and *ever*

Visuals:

V1	Manuel and Jenny Vega are senior citizens. They are always active.
V2	They usually go to the community center on weekdays to meet their friends.
V3	They often go on field trips to interesting places in the city.
V4	They rarely stay home and sit around.
V5	They seldom argue with each other.
V6	They never go to bed angry.
V7	Let's Talk: We Rarely Have Lunch There

Page 2

✔Opening: Your Daily Routine

1. Give examples of things you do often. Ask a few students questions to elicit the same.

2. Ask students how their daily routines have changed since coming to this country. You might want to teach "used to" for talking about past habits.

3. Have students form groups of 3–5 and discuss their daily routines and how their lifestyles have changed since coming to this country.

Something New: How Often?

1. Briefly explain lesson objectives.

2. Show V1–V6 and tell the story in the text while students listen.

3. Model the sentences and have students repeat.

4. Show each visual and ask questions with "How often?" for class, then individuals to answer.

Practice: "They go to meet their friends"

1. Show the first visual and ask questions with *ever, usually*, etc. to generate statements about Manuel and Jenny.

2. Have volunteers form questions about the picture for class to answer.

 3. Have students open books and read individually and/or in pairs what has been practiced orally in the Something New and Practice sections.

Let's Talk: We Rarely Have Lunch There*

1. Use the dialogue visual to establish the context of the conversation.

2. Model the dialogue as students listen, indicating the speakers by pointing to the visual or other means.

3. Model the dialogue again and ask comprehension questions.

4. Model the dialogue and have class repeat.

5. Take one role and have class take the other role; then change roles.

6. Divide class in half and have them take the two roles; then have them switch roles.

7. Have volunteers say the dialogue for the class.

 8. Have class open books and practice the dialogue in pairs.

*Cassette users can have students listen to the dialogue first with books closed.

Practice: "How often do you go?"

1. Ask individuals questions with "How often?" and then ask the class, "How often does he/she _____?" about each answer to practice the third person singular form.

 2. Have class open books and read the Practice in pairs.

3. Have pairs who finish quickly ask and answer their own questions.

Practice Activity: I often watch TV in the evening

1. Model example sentences. Form groups of 3–6 students and have groups make up sentences.

2. Bring the class together and start a chain drill: S1 asks S2 a question with "How often," S2 answers and asks S3, S3 answers and asks S4, and on around the room as the whole class listens.

Page 6 ## Something New: Safety

1. Have students look at the illustrations in the book and model the safety reminders using *always* and *never*. (Optional: Use a transparency of the page so you can show each illustration before the words. Elicit the ideas from the class as you show the illustrations.)

2. Elicit from the class additional safety reminders using *always* and *never*.

3. Have pairs read the Something New and the following Practice: "Always turn the water off."

Page 7 ## ★ Something Extra: Sometimes

1. Have students look at the illustration in the text as you read the sentences.

2. Ask comprehension questions.

3. Have students read independently.

Page 8 ## ★ Something Extra: Do You Ever…?

Ask the whole class and/or individuals the questions given and similar questions. Model the short answer for each.

☛ Practice: "No, never"

Have students open books and practice in pairs. They can continue the Practice with their own "Do you ever…" questions.

☛ Practice Activity: Always and Never

1. Form groups of 4–6 students. Demonstrate by writing on the chalkboard the words *always* and *never* with space for a column under each. Have one member of each group do the same on a sheet of paper.

2. Have students make a list of items for the group under each column. Complete sentences are not required.

3. Have students ask each other questions about the list as in the example, and answer using a short answer with *always, never, usually*, etc.

Page 9 ## 🔊 Reading: A Creature of Habit*

1. Have students read silently or read the story aloud to them.

2. Ask comprehension questions and then have students read the story again.

3. Initiate discussion by asking whole class and/or individuals the questions.

4. Have students continue the discussion in pairs or groups.

*Cassette users can have students listen to the Reading first with books closed.

✍ Writing

1. Elicit 5–6 sentences on one student's daily routine.

2. Elicit other activities students would do in their daily routines.

3. Have students write their own daily routines.

4. Have volunteers read their paragraphs to the class.

Lesson 25 Activity Pages

Page 10 **A. Listen to Elena tell about her life. Write one of the vocabulary words in the space under each picture.***

1. Go over the directions with students. Review vocabulary. Discuss illustrations if you wish. Read script or play tape, repeating as often as necessary, until students have filled in all the spaces.

Script:
I'm what you call an *all or nothing* woman. I either always do something, or I never do it. For example:

I clean my house and invite someone to eat dinner with me every Saturday. I always do that. I enjoy cooking, and it always makes me feel good.

I never smoke at home. I don't want to smell up my nice house, and I don't want my children to have to breathe smoke.

I turn the lights out when I leave the room so I can save energy. At least I usually do. I try to. It saves me money, too.

When I get good news, I never celebrate. I don't eat. I don't drink or go out. I just put the money in the bank instead.

If I feel tired, I force myself to go to school anyway. I always go to school. I'm afraid that if I don't go once, I will get lazy.

2. Check student work by having volunteers say the answers. Encourage them to speak as much as possible by asking "Elena always…?" etc.

*Cassette users can have students listen to the script on the tape.

B. Arrange these words in order from most frequent to least frequent.
Go over the directions with the students. Have them start with "always" as the first word on the left, working their way to "never" on the right. Explain that if two words mean the same thing they can be placed one above the other.

C. Compare your list with your partner's.
Have pairs compare their answers to B above and discuss.

Page 11
D. Fill in the blanks with the vocabulary words.
1. Go over directions with students. Discuss vocabulary related to the illustration of a sky–diver and a rock climber.

2. Ask a volunteer or two to read the story once students have filled in the blanks.

3. Discuss the story if you wish. Students might enjoy telling about themselves.

Losing Things

Communication Objectives:
Report a lost card
Get information about replacing a lost card
Agree and disagree

New Structures:
Future with *will*

Visuals:
V8   driver's license
V9   residence card
V10   credit card
V11   Social Security card
V12   Let's Talk: When Will I Get My Duplicate License?

Page 12

✔ Review: Do You Ever...?

1. Give examples of things you do in your free time. Ask a few students questions to elicit the same.

2. Give examples of hobbies. Tell about a hobby you or someone you know has. Ask a few students questions to elicit the same.

Something New: Identification Cards and Credit Cards

1. Briefly explain lesson objectives: To learn what to do if you lose your driver's license or credit cards.

2. Show V8–V11, model the vocabulary, and have students repeat.

3. Show each visual and ask questions with "What...?" and "Who has a...?" for the class, then individuals, to answer.

Page 13

Something New: Sara Lost Her Wallet

1. Ask students what is happening in the picture. Tell the story.

2. Have students read silently or read the story aloud to them.

3. Ask comprehension questions and then have students read the story again.

Discussion

Initiate discussion by asking whole class and/or individuals the questions. Discuss how to replace a driver's license or ID card in your state.

Page 14 **Let's Talk:** When Will I Get My Duplicate License?*

1. Use the dialogue visual to establish the context of the conversation.

2. Model the dialogue as students listen, indicating the speakers by pointing to the visual or other means.

3. Model the dialogue again and ask comprehension questions.

4. Model the dialogue and have class repeat.

5. Take one role and have class take other role; then change roles.

6. Divide class in half and have them take the two roles; then have them switch roles.

7. Have volunteers say the dialogue for the class.

 8. Have class open books and practice the dialogue in pairs.

*Cassette users can have students listen to the dialogue first with books closed.

☛ Practice: "When?"

 1. Ask individuals questions with *will* and note on the board the future time expressions they use.

2. Explain the future time expressed with *next* _____, *by* _____, and *in* _____.

 3. Have students open books and practice in pairs.

Page 15 ### ☛ Practice Activity: What does Sara need to do?

1. Review Let's Talk: When Will I Get My Duplicate Driver's License? with the students.

2. Have students fill in the blanks to complete the three conversations on their own.

3. Correct orally or have volunteers write the answers on an overhead transparency of page 15.

☛ **Practice Activity: I lost my Social Security card**

Go over directions with students. Have them find new partners for each conversation.

Page 16 🎝 **Reading:** Always Losing Something*

1. Have students read silently or read the story aloud to them.

2. Ask comprehension questions and then have students read the story again.

*Cassette users can have students listen to the Reading first with books closed.

✍ **Writing**

1. Write example #1 on the chalkboard. Read it. Ask the class if it's true. Write their answer: "Yes, she is." Read sentence #1 again. Ask if they agree. Write the answer, "I agree."

2. Write example #2 on the chalkboard. Repeat procedure above for this example.

3. Instruct students to write their answers for #1–6.

4. Check orally by reading the statements and having students give their answers.

Lesson 26 Activity Pages

Page 17 🎝 ***A. Listen to the gypsy foretell the future. Put the correct number under the picture.****

1. Go over the directions with the class to make sure that students understand that they need to listen to the script and write the number of the description that matches the picture.

2. Play the tape as often as is necessary for all the students to answer the questions. If you don't have a tape, read the script at normal conversational speed.

Script:
My name is Clara the Magnificent. Now, I will look into my crystal ball, where I will see the future.

1. Oh, I see very good things in the future for you. You will find a good husband, get married, and have a very happy family.

2. Now, let's look at you. You are very ambitious. You work hard. You will be a very successful business executive.

3. Hmmm…It's difficult for me to tell about you. I see religion. You will be a religious leader, maybe a priest. Your work will be in a church. I can see that.

4. You will go for a high school diploma. After that, it will be a college degree. You are an excellent student because you study.

5. I…don't want to tell you what I see. It's not good. You will be in the hospital. Well, wait a minute. No, you won't have to go to the hospital because you quit smoking. That's great! You made me nervous for a minute.

*Cassette users can have students listen to the script on the tape.

B. Partner 1 look at this page. Partner 2 look at D on Page 18.
Go over directions with class. Examine the resolutions. Remind Partner 2 that his/her part is on the next page.

Page 18

C. Find someone in the class who can write his/her name in the space.
1. Go over directions with students. Ask class how you would form questions: e.g., You need to say, "Will you change apartments this year?"

2. Have students stand up, walk around the room, and ask the questions. When they get a *yes* answer, that person will print his/her name in the space.

D. Partner 2 look at this page. Partner 1 look at B on page 17.
See B above.

Using the Telephone

Communication Objectives:

Identify numbers to call for telephone information and services

Spell names aloud

Confirm instructions using *will*

Write a telephone message

Find a problem on a telephone bill

New Structures:

Will to confirm or agree

Visuals:

V13   Dial 411 for Directory Assistance (Information)

V14   Dial 611 for telephone repair

V15   Dial 011 for a different country

V16   Dial 0 for a collect call or a credit card call

V17   Dial 00 for a long distance operator

V18   Let's Talk: What City, Please?

V19   Let's Talk: Take a Message

Page 20

✔ Review: I Lost My...

1. Give an example of something important you, or someone you know, that was lost. Ask a few students question #1 to elicit the same.

2. Give an example of the last thing you lost. Tell what you did about it.

3. Have students form groups of 3–5. Each student then tells the others the saddest story they ever heard about someone who lost something. Then each student tells the others the last thing they lost and what they did about it.

Something New: Telephone Services

1. Briefly explain lesson objectives: To use the telephone to get information.

2. Show V13–V17 and tell the story in the text while students listen.

3. Model the sentences and have students repeat.

4. Show each visual and ask questions such as, "What number do you call...?" for class, then individuals, to answer.

Page 21   **Let's Talk:** What City, Please?*

 1. Use the dialogue visual to establish the context of the conversation.

2. Model the dialogue as students listen, indicating the speakers by pointing to the visual or other means.

3. Model the dialogue again and ask comprehension questions.

4. Model the dialogue and have class repeat.

5. Take one role and have class take the other; then change roles.

6. Divide class in half and have them take the two roles; then have them switch roles.

7. Have volunteers say the dialogue for the class.

 8. Have class open books and practice the dialogue in pairs.

*Cassette users can have students listen to the dialogue first with books closed.

Page 22 **☛ Practice: "What city, please?"**

1. Have class read the Practice in pairs.

2. Have pairs who finish quickly ask and answer their own questions.

☛ Practice Activity: Spelling Your Name

 1. Model the example dialogue, indicating the words *tomato, sing,* and *up* on the board.

2. Write the name "Tsu" on the board. Write "T" next to "tomato," etc.

3. Explain that to spell a name, people sometimes use this method: A as in apple; B as in boy, etc. (as shown in text).

4. Model the dialogue again and ask comprehension questions.

5. As a class, make a chart of words for each letter of the alphabet. (You might want to go around the room and let everyone select one word for the chart.)

6. Have students practice spelling their own names using the chart.

★ Something Extra: Wrong Numbers

1. Ask students what they say when they call a wrong number.

2. Have a student volunteer demonstrate calling a wrong number. For fun, you might prepare an index card for the student to read:

Student: (Dials) Hello, Mother?
Teacher: No.
Student: I'm sorry.

3. Review the expressions: "I'm sorry" and "Excuse me."

4. Ask students what they say when they receive a wrong number.

5. Have a student volunteer demonstrate receiving a wrong number:

Teacher: Hello, is this the White House?
Student: I think you have the wrong number.

☛ Practice Activity: I'm sorry

1. Have pairs practice calling wrong numbers. Tell Partner A to think of someone they want to call. Model: "I'd like to speak to…" Tell Partner B to think of the answer. Model: "I think you have the wrong number…" Etc.

2. Have students practice the dialogue above.

3. Have students reverse roles.

Let's Talk: Take a Message

1. Show the visual and ask students to describe what they think is going on.

2. Model the dialogue as students listen, indicating the speakers by pointing to the visual or other means.

3. Model the dialogue again and ask comprehension questions.

4. Model the dialogue and have class repeat.

5. Take one role and have class take other role; then change roles.

6. Divide class in half and have them take the two roles; then have them switch roles.

7. Have volunteers say the dialogue for the class.

 8. Have class open books and practice the dialogue in pairs.

Page 24 ☛ **Practice: "Okay, I will"**

1. Have class read the Practice in pairs.

2. Have pairs who finish quickly ask and answer their own questions about missing or incorrect information on a telephone message.

☛ **Practice Activity: He's out right now**

1. Ask students what a cable company does and what a receptionist does. Explain that they are going to read and write information from a receptionist's telephone conversation.

2. Model the dialogue.

3. Have students practice in pairs.

4. Make overhead transparency of telephone message.

5. Ask "who" and "what" comprehension questions about the dialogue. Fill in (or have a student volunteer fill in) the blanks on the transparency. (Note: Students can put today's day and time on the message. They should write, "before 5:30" on the message line and check the space next to "please call.")

Page 25 📼 **Reading:** A Telephone Bill*

1. Discuss the illustration of an excerpt from a telephone bill. Go over the abbreviations, making sure everything is clear. You might want to do this with an overhead transparency of the illustration.

2. Have the students read silently or read the story aloud to them.

3. Ask comprehension questions and then have students read the story again.

4. Initiate discussion by asking whole class and/or individuals questions about their phone bills, if desired.

*Cassette users can have students listen to the Reading first with books closed.

Page 26   ✐ **Writing**

1. Have students read all the questions and then write their answers, from the story above, in the blanks.

2. Check student answers orally.

Lesson 27 Activity Pages

Page 27 🔲 **A. Listen to the telephone call and fill in the blanks.***

1. Go over the directions to make sure that students understand that they need to listen to the dialogue and fill in the form.

2. Go over the form before playing or reading the dialogue. (Note: When dialogues have more than one character and you don't have a tape, you may want to ask volunteers to read the script.)

Script:

Store Clerk: Katie's Clothes Store.

Caller: This is Ben Galloway. May I speak to Katie?

Store Clerk: She's not here. May I take a message?

Caller: Yes. Please tell her Ben Galloway of Galloway and Associates called.

Store Clerk: Can you spell your last name, please?

Caller: Yes. G–A–L–L–O–W–A–Y.

Store Clerk: Your number?

Caller: Three one oh, nine eight seven, nine eight seven nine. Tell her I returned her call.

Store Clerk: I will.

Caller: Thanks. Bye.

Store Clerk: Goodbye.

*Cassette users can have students listen to the script on the tape.

B. Match the numbers dialed with the conversations.
Go over the directions.

Page 28   ### C. Fill in the blanks with the vocabulary words in the box.
1. Review vocabulary words.

2. Have students do exercise individually or in pairs.

3. Have students correct with a partner or as a class. As an optional extension activity, have students practice dialogue, taking turns at both roles.

Unit Nine | Evaluation

Page 29 ***I. Listening Comprehension****

    1. Go over the directions for Part I with students.

    2. Read each item of the script two times, at normal conversational speed.

        Script:
        1. They often visit interesting places.

        2. They seldom argue.

        3. I usually wash my hair in the shower.

        4. I always unplug the iron.

        5. Tai lost his residence card.

        6. Next time I will ask how to spell his name.

        7. It's a toll–free call.

        8. You talked 14 minutes.

    *Cassette users can have students listen to the script on the tape.

Page 30 ***II. Reading and III. Writing***

    1. Go over the directions for Parts II and III with students.

    2. Have class do these sections independently.

Evaluation Check

    1. Correct evaluation by having student volunteers write their answers on the board or on an overhead transparency.

    2. Have class check their answers.

    3. Circulate to make sure students have checked their work accurately.

Weekend Specials

Communication Objectives:
Talk about quantities of food
Discuss specials and sales
Read coupons

New Structures:
Count and non–count nouns
Partitives: *a bunch of, a can of*, etc.

Visuals:

V20	bananas
V21	two bananas
V22	apples
V23	three apples
V24	cucumbers
V25	one cucumber
V26	milk
V27	a carton of milk
V28	coffee
V29	a can of coffee
V30	cereal
V31	two boxes of cereal
V32	Let's Talk: Thomas' Shopping List

Other instructional aids: Real coupons

Page 32

✔ Review

Telephone Services

1. Ask questions about what you can and can't find out by phone.

2. Ask volunteers to give your local numbers for time, information and weather.

Spelling Your Name

In a chain drill, have students practice spelling their last names.

Something New: Count and Non–Count Words

1. Briefly explain lesson objectives: To talk about food and marketing.

2. Show visuals V21–V31 and explain while students listen. Use V20 and V21 and say "We can count *bananas*. We can say two *bananas*." Repeat procedure for V22–V23 and V24–V25.

3. Use V26 and V27 and say "We can't count *milk*. We must say *a carton of milk*." Repeat procedure for V28–V29 and V30–V31.

4. Model the language for all the visuals again and have students repeat.

5. Show each visual and ask, "Can we count this/these?" for class, then individuals, to answer.

Page 34 **Let's Talk:** Tomas' Shopping List*

1. Use the dialogue visual to establish the context of the conversation.

2. Model the dialogue as students listen, indicating the speakers and foods by pointing to visual or other means.

3. Model the dialogue again and ask comprehension questions.

4. Model the dialogue and have class repeat.

5. Take one role and have class take other role; then change roles.

6. Divide class in half and have them take the two roles; then have them switch roles.

7. Have volunteers say the dialogue for the class.

 8. Have class open books and practice the dialogue in pairs.

*Cassette users can have students listen to the dialogue first with books closed.

☛ **Practice: "What do we need?"**

 1. Ask individuals questions with "What do they need?" Then ask individuals "What do you need/want?" Then ask the class, "What does he/she____?" to practice the third person singular form.

 2. Have class open books and read the Practice in pairs.

3. Have pairs who finish quickly ask and answer their own questions.

Page 35 ☛ **Practice: "How much shrimp do you want?"**

 Have students read the Practice section in pairs.

☛ **Practice Activity: Marketing**

    1. Have pairs make shopping lists.

    2. Ask volunteers to read their shopping lists. Ask class to say whether each item is count or non–count.

    3. Go over the directions for the pair practice and ask a volunteer pair to demonstrate.

    4. Have students practice in pairs.

📼 **Reading:** What's On Sale?*

    1. Have students read silently or read the story aloud to them.

    2. Ask comprehension questions and then have students read the story again.

    3. Initiate discussion by asking whole class and/or individuals the questions.

    4. Have students discuss in pairs or in groups.

    *Cassette users can have students listen to the Reading first with books closed.

✍ **Writing**

    1. Read the information about what Tomas bought to the students.

    2. Instruct students to fill in the blanks with vocabulary from the paragraph above.

    3. Read item #1 with the class. Ask, "How much or how many?" Read, "He bought…" and elicit the answer from the class.

    4. Write question and answer to #1 on the board or on a transparency.

    5. Instruct students to complete #2–5.

    6. Check answers on the board or transparency.

★ **Something Extra:** Discount Coupons

    1. If possible, prepare an overhead transparency of the coupons.

    2. Explain each coupon, indicating illustrations and explaining vocabulary.

    3. Read coupons to class.

4. (Optional) Show real coupons that you have brought in, read them to the class, and then pass them around for students to read.

Page 38 ## Discussion

1. Read questions #1–3 and elicit answers from volunteers.

2. When discussing #3, elicit specific coupons students look for, receive, use, or might use.

☞ Practice: "When does this coupon expire?"

1. Ask whole class and/or individuals the questions given and similar questions. Model the short answer for each.

2. Have students practice in pairs.

☞ Practice Activity: Home Assignment

Refer students back to the Discussion where they talked about where to get coupons. Ask individuals what coupons they can bring. Encourage each student to bring a coupon or two.

Lesson 28 Activity Page

Page 39 **A. Listen to the checker check Maria's groceries. Write the name of the container in the space.***

Go over the directions with class to make sure that students understand that they need to listen to the dialogue and write the correct word in each space as they hear it.

Script:

Checker: How are you today, Maria?

Maria: Fine. But I hope I have enough money for these groceries.

Checker: Don't worry. Let's see what you have…. This bag of potato chips is a dollar forty–nine a bag today. The milk's eighty–nine cents a carton. My family drinks eight cartons a week!

Maria: Wow! That's a lot!

Checker: Scallions are thirty–nine cents a bunch. I remember when a bunch was fifteen cents.

Maria: You're not that old.

Checker:	I am! One bottle of Sam's Salad Dressing. Is this bottled stuff any good?
Maria:	The kids like it.
Checker:	Six cans of tomato sauce at nineteen cents a can… two boxes of cereal.
Maria:	Just give me one box.
Checker:	Okay. That's nine eighteen. Do you have enough money?
Maria:	…Yes! I made it. Here's a ten.

*Cassette users can have students listen to the script on the tape.

B. Can you count these foods? Check yes or no.
1. Direct students, working individually or in pairs, to check *yes* or *no*. (If necessary, review what count and non–count means.)

2. Circulate or go on to exercise C to check for answers.

C. Look at your "No" column above.
1. Explain to students that they need to read the "No" column in B section above for their answers. For example, we can't count milk. Therefore, we talk about it as a carton or pitcher of milk as shown in exercise C, #1.

2. Students can work as individuals or in pairs. Partners can check each other, or you can check answers as a class.

D. Discuss with your partner.
Have students answer in pairs or as a class.

To Market, To Market

Communication Objectives:
> Locate items in a supermarket
> Select from various kinds of food stores

New Structures:
> *Some* and *any*

Visuals:
> V33   Dale's Market
> V34   Aisle 1
> V35   Aisle 2
> V36   Aisle 3
> V37   Aisle 4
> V38   Aisle 5
> V39   Let's Talk: We're All Sold Out

Page 40 ✔ **Review:** Coupons

> 1. If a few students brought in coupons, or if you have some, read them aloud to the class and then pass them around.

> 2. If you have enough coupons, form groups of 4–5 students and have them read and compare several coupons per group as directed in the text.

Something New: Dale's Market

> 1. Briefly explain lesson objectives: To locate items in a supermarket.

> 2. Show visuals V33–V38, model the vocabulary while students listen.

> 3. Model the vocabulary and have students repeat.

> 4. Ask comprehension questions for class, then individuals, to answer.

Page 41 **Let's Talk:** We're All Sold Out*

> 1. Use the dialogue visual to establish the context of the conversation.

> 2. Model the dialogue as students listen, indicating the speakers by pointing to the visual or other means.

3. Model the dialogue again and ask comprehension questions.

4. Model the dialogue and have class repeat.

5. Take one role and have class take the other role; then change roles.

6. Divide class in half and have them take the two roles; then have them switch roles.

7. Have volunteers say the dialogue for the class.

 8. Have class open books and practice the dialogue in pairs.

*Cassette users can have students listen to the dialogue first with books closed.

☛ Practice: "Can I help you?"

 1. Ask individuals, "Can I help you?" and have them tell you what they're looking for. Then direct them to an aisle or section of the store.

 2. Have class open books and read the Practice in pairs. Note: In your region you may say "in aisle 3" instead of "on aisle 3." If so, explain and have students change it in their books.

3. Have pairs who finish quickly ask and answer their own questions.

Page 42 ## ☛ Practice Activity: Where can I find beans?

 1. As a class, make up a marketing list on the chalkboard from various departments: e.g., hamburger, onions, chili pepper.

2. Show visual of Dale's Market. Ask class where they would find chili pepper. Elicit the answer, "Aisle 3." Ask "Why?" Answer: "Spices are on Aisle 3. Chili pepper is a spice."

3. Model example Practice with a volunteer student. Then practice example with class.

 4. Refer students to page 40 with the visual of Dale's Market. Instruct students to use the class shopping list on the board and the visual on page 40 to do the Practice Activity.

★ Something Extra: Some and Any

1. Instruct students to look at illustration and discuss the conversation.

2. Explain that we use "some" when we expect the answer to be affirmative; "any" when the response is negative. Model a few sentences like "I'd like *some* sugar" and "I don't want *any* cream." Then model questions with *some, any, somewhere, anywhere, something, anything,* etc.

Page 43

☞ Practice: "Do you want some?"

1. Have students read individually and/or in pairs the Something Extra and Practice sections.

2. Have pairs practice the conversations. Those who finish quickly should look at the pictures and try to say the dialogues from memory.

☞ Practice Activity: Find the Categories

1. Direct students again to page 40 while you show the visual of Dale's Market.

2. Form groups of 3 or 4. Have students write the aisle # on the space next to the product. For example, "paper napkins" would be found on Aisle #4. Students should write a "4" in the space. (Note: You might want to time this exercise and make it a contest between groups.)

3. Discuss different answers as a class.

Page 44

📼 Reading: The Convenience Store*

1. Have students read silently or read the story aloud to them.

2. Ask comprehension questions and then have students read the story again.

3. Initiate discussion by asking whole class and/or individuals the questions.

*Cassette users can have students listen to the Reading first with books closed.

Discussion

Have students discuss in groups or pairs.

✍ Writing

1. Students fill in the blanks with *some* or *any.* They may work as individuals and then check their answers in pairs, groups, or as a class.

2. Encourage students to read the complete sentences aloud after they have filled in the blanks to check their work and for practice.

Page 45 **A. Follow Yolanda on her shopping trip. Draw her trip around the store with your pencil.***

    1. Go over the floor plan with students; then go over the directions and make sure that they understand where to start and how to draw the line showing Yolanda's path around the store.

    2. Play the tape or read the script.

        Script:

        Yolanda just invited her boyfriend to dinner. She's going to make salmon pasta and a salad, and have bread, wine and dessert. She goes in, gets a cart and heads left past aisle 1 to the seafood section at the back of the store. She picks up some salmon and keeps going along the back to aisle three. She turns down aisle three and picks up some pasta. She goes back down aisle 4 and turns right to the dairy wall. She picks up some cream for the salmon sauce. Now she has the ingredients for her salmon pasta. For the salad, she goes to the right to the produce section on the right wall. She gets a head of lettuce, a bunch of scallions, some tomatoes and a bunch of cilantro. She goes across to aisle ten for a bottle of salad dressing. Then she goes back to the bakery (next to produce) in the back of the store. Once she has her bread, she goes across the back of the store to aisle seven for a bottle of white wine. For ice cream, she makes a U–turn at the front of the store and goes to the frozen foods on aisle five. Finished, she turns around and goes to the checkout counter, pays for her groceries, and exits out the same door she came in.

    *Cassette users can have students listen to the script on tape.

B. Discuss stores with your partner. Ask, "Where do you shop most?"
Have students discuss where they shop for food and why.

C. Write your partner's answer and why.

    1. Have individuals write down what they found out about their partners.

    2. Volunteers can read their answers to the class, or partners can check each other's answers.

D. Partner 1 look at this page and partner 2 look at G on page 47.
Explain the directions for activity to class.

1. For this activity, review what a coupon is for and what kind of information is written on a coupon.

2. Direct students to work in pairs. Have each student in the pair working on a different page (Partner 1's on page 46, Partner 2's on page 47).

3. Have pairs take turns asking questions about the missing information in their grid; then fill in the grid with the information their partners give them.

E. Fill in the blanks with the correct word.
Students can do this activity individually or in pairs. Give the usual directions, go over vocabulary, have students do exercise, and check in pairs or as a class.

F. Write about food you have and don't have in your refrigerator. Use "any" or "some."
Explain that students will complete these sentences by writing what they have or don't have in their own refrigerators at home. Volunteers can read answers to the class or the teacher can check answers.

G. Partner 2 look at this page and partner 1 look at D on page 46.
See D above.

Lesson 30

A Pizza Party

Communication Objectives:
> Talk about preparing food
> Consider a household budget

New Structures:
> Quantifiers: *a little, a few*, and *a lot of*

Visuals:
> V40   a few tomatoes
> V41   a few mushrooms
> V42   a few meatballs
> V43   a little tomato sauce
> V44   a little sausage
> V45   a little oregano
> V46   a lot of cheese
> V47   Let's Talk: Don't Forget the Cheese

Page 48

✔ Review: At the Market

1. Looking at page 40, orient students for "Where can I find…" "They're on aisle…" conversation.

2. Demonstrate example. Let students practice in pairs or as a class.

3. Tell class about your favorite convenience store: e.g., what it's called, where it's located, what you buy there, when, etc. Ask volunteers to do same.

4. Tell why you like your convenience store. Ask volunteers to do same.

Something New: Let's Make Pizza!

1. Briefly explain lesson objectives: To talk about making food for a party.

2. Show V40–V46 and tell the story in the text while students listen.

3. Model the sentences and have students repeat.

4. Show each visual and ask, "What are these?" or "What's this?" for class, then individuals, to answer.

Page 49 **Let's Talk:** Don't Forget the Cheese*

 1. Use the dialogue visual to establish the context of the conversation.

2. Model the dialogue as students listen, indicating the speakers by pointing to the visual or other means.

3. Model the dialogue again and ask comprehension questions.

4. Model the dialogue and have class repeat.

5. Take one role and have class take other role; then change roles.

6. Divide class in half and have them take the two roles; then have them switch roles.

7. Have volunteers say the dialogue for the class.

 8. Have class open books and practice the dialogue in pairs.

*Cassette users can have students listen to the dialogue first with books closed.

Page 50 ☛ **Practice: "What would you like?"**

 1. Ask individuals, "What would you like?" Then ask the class, "What would he/she like?" using each answer to practice *a little*, *a lot*, and *a few*.

 2. Have class open books and read the Practice in pairs.

3. Have pairs who finish quickly ask and answer their own questions.

☛ **Practice Activity: A Green Salad**

1. Talk about making a green salad and elicit from the class all the ingredients they can think of.

 2. Tell students the names of two or three other salads. Form groups and ask each group to choose a salad they like.

3. Have everyone in the group list all the ingredients they can think of for their salad.

4. Have students take turns telling what quantity they want in the salad using *a few*, *a little*, and *a lot*.

5. Have a group representative tell or write on the board his/her group's list of ingredients for their salad.

★ Something Extra: A Party

1. Make an overhead of the party pictures. Cover the vocabulary on the right. Ask class to describe the top picture with vocabulary they already know. Make sure they notice the time.

2. Read the language that goes with the picture. Note that "a lot of" is used with both count and non–count nouns.

3. Have students repeat.

4. Ask comprehension questions, "Is there a lot of food?" etc.

5. Repeat procedure for second and third pictures.

 6. Have students open books and discuss party at 7:00, 10:00 and 12 o'clock. Then instruct students to cover the language on the right side of the page and continue to practice.

☞ Practice Activity: Our classroom

1. Model the same sentences as in Something Extra with items in your classroom. Say, "In our classroom, we have a lot of…" (Provide class with vocabulary as necessary.) Instruct students to fill in the blanks in their books.

3. Have students compare their answers with their partner's.

🔊 Reading: A Household Budget*

1. Have students read silently or read the story aloud to them.

2. Ask comprehension questions and then have students read the story again.

3. Initiate discussion by asking whole class and/or individuals the questions. Have students discuss in pairs or groups.

*Cassette users can have students listen to the Reading first with books closed.

✍ Writing

1. Instruct students to fill in the blanks with the vocabulary words.

2. Read the first sentences, allowing class to volunteer the correct vocabulary.

3. Correct answers as a class.

Page 54 **A. Listen and check the amount.***

> 1. Go over the grid. Give directions explaining that students need to listen to the dialogue and check under the correct column.
>
> 2. Play the tape or read the script.

> **Script:**
> As we all know, different friends have different interests. Janie just went away to college. She called her mother and, of course, her mother wants to know about her new friends. Listen to Janie describe her friends to her mother.

> Janie: I don't have many new friends, mother, but I have a few. A few really nice people...girls—and boys... Jerry has a lot of interest in art. He paints and draws a lot. He even drew a picture of me...my face. He drew my face.
> Then there's Bill, a guy in my history class. He has a few different interests. He likes history, of course, but he likes a few other things, too, like business—and maybe he'll study law...
> Yeah, Jean, she's my roommate. She's extremely considerate and nice, cute, but a little messy and a little busy. Haven't seen a lot of her...no, it's not because of my boyfriends...it's not.

> *Cassette users can have students listen to the script on the tape.

B. Change the statements to "Do you have...?" questions.

> 1. Go over the list to clarify vocabulary.
>
> 2. Model how to ask the questions.
>
> 3. Go over the directions. Explain that nobody can sign the same list twice, and that everybody has to get up, move around the room and find students to sign their paper. You might want to give a prize to the winner(s) and make it a timed exercise. This often adds more tension and fun to the activity.

Page 55 **C. Help your partner plan a party.**

> 1. Explain that students need to fill in the blanks with *How much* or *How many* at the beginning of the sentence and than ask their partners the questions.
>
> 2. As partner answers, the interviewer writes his/her partner's answers in the space at the end of the question.
>
> 3. Correct as a class or have partners switch papers.

Evaluation

Page 57 **I. Listening Comprehension***

    1. Go over the directions for Part I with students.

    2. Read each item of the script two times, at normal conversational speed.

> **Script:**
> 1. How many did you buy?
>
> 2. How much do you want?
>
> 3. I'm sorry. We're all sold out.
>
> 4. Suzanne saved $1.79.
>
> 5. It's in the meat section.
>
> 6. Where's the rice? It's on aisle 3.
>
> 7. It has more weekend specials.
>
> 8. I'm looking at my budget.

    *Cassette users can have students listen to the script on the tape.

Page 58 **II. Reading and III. Writing**

    1. Go over the directions for Parts II and III with students.

    2. Have class do these sections independently.

Evaluation Check

    1. Correct evaluation by having student volunteers write their answers on the board or an overhead transparency.

    2. Have class check their answers.

    3. Circulate to make sure students have checked their work accurately.

Unit Eleven | Lesson 31

Who's Older? Who's Younger?

Communication Objectives:
  Compare children's ages
  Select babysitters

New Structures:
  Comparative adjectives: *–er* form
  Old enough to

Visuals:
  V48   The Sanders Children
  V49   The Kim Children
  V50   Let's Talk: We Need a Babysitter

Page 60

✔ Review: A Few and a Little

Tell class you want to order a pizza. Ask what they want. Elicit answers from volunteers using the vocabulary: *a little, a lot, a few, much* or *many*.

Something New: Families

1. Briefly explain lesson objectives: To talk about children's ages.

2. Show V48–V49, and model the sentences while students listen.

3. Model the sentences and have students repeat.

4. Show each visual and ask questions with, "Is _____ older/younger than _____?" for class, then individuals, to answer.

Page 61

☛ Practice: "Jimmy is older than Amy"

1. Write the first and last names and the ages of all the children on the board.

2. Have individuals volunteer to say one match (i.e., "Amy is younger than Jimmy.") to the class. Correct if necessary.

3. Have pairs make up as many sentences as they can for five minutes, alternating between Partner 1 and Partner 2.

☛ Practice: "This is my younger child"

1. Use an overhead transparency of this Practice to model the four conversations if you think it will be helpful.

2. Practice as a class.

3. Have students practice the dialogues in pairs.

☛ Practice Activity: My Family

1. Draw a picture of your family on the chalkboard. Talk about your family using "older/younger than" and "He's/She's 14," etc.

2. Have students draw pictures of their own families in the space provided.

3. Have students share their drawings and talk about their families in groups.

  ## Let's Talk: We Need a Babysitter*

1. Use the dialogue visual to establish the context of the conversation.

2. Model the dialogue as students listen, indicating the speakers by pointing to the visual or other means.

3. Model the dialogue again and ask comprehension questions.

4. Model the dialogue and have class repeat.

5. Take one role and have class take other role; then change roles.

6. Divide class in half and have them take the two roles; then have them switch roles.

7. Have volunteers say the dialogue for the class.

 8. Have class open books and practice the dialogue in pairs.

*Cassette users can have students listen to the dialogue first with books closed.

Discussion

1. Identify people in class who have children.

2. Have other students ask them the Discussion questions.

Page 64

★ Something Extra: Is She Old Enough?

1. Have students look at pictures. Ask class questions about the ages of Lucy, Joe, and Mr. Green.

2. Have students repeat a few questions to prepare for the activity.

3. Have groups of students take turns asking and answering questions about Lucy, Joe, and Mr. Green.

4. Regroup students as a class. Ask volunteers to say why Lucy is old enough (or not) to babysit, etc.

Page 65

★ Something Extra: I'm Happier Than I Was Earlier

1. Use the illustration in the text to establish the context.

2. Model the dialogue as students listen and read along.

3. Have students listen and repeat.

4. Point out the spelling of the *–er* form in an adjective that ends in *–y*.

5. Have students practice the dialogue in pairs.

☛ Practice: "He's friendlier than he used to be"

1. Ask individuals questions using *earlier, happier, friendlier, easier*, etc.

2. Have class read the Practice in pairs.

3. Pairs who finish quickly can ask and answer their own questions.

4. Ask students how they changed *early* to *earlier, happy* to *happier*, etc. Discuss.

5. Have students fill in the blanks. Have volunteers write the words on the chalkboard to check spelling.

Page 66

📼 Reading: Minors and Adults*

1. Have students read silently or read the story aloud to them.

2. Ask comprehension questions and then have students read the story again.

3. Initiate discussion by asking whole class and/or individuals the questions on page 67.

4. Have students continue the discussion in pairs or groups.

*Cassette users can have students listen to the Reading first with books closed.

Page 67   ✐ **Writing**

1. Go over directions. Review the *–ier* ending.

2. Have students fill in the blanks for #1–6.

3. Check by asking student volunteers to spell their answers.

4. Instruct students to write three sentences about themselves. Demonstrate by writing a sentence about yourself on the board.

5. Invite volunteers to read their sentences aloud.

Lesson 31 Activity Pages

Page 68   *A. Listen and circle the word you hear.**

1. Go over vocabulary in lists. Go over directions. Explain that students will listen to the dialogue and circle the word that best describes the person talking.

2. Play the tape or read the script.

Script:
1. He's tall, dark and handsome, but I'm cuter. Everyone says I'm the cute one.

2. I hate to be late, but today I'm later than ever.

3. He's wealthier than most anyone around here. A lot of people have money, but he's just plain wealthy.

4. They are checking to see who's taller. Jane says she's the tall one, and Jerry says he is.

5. Jill didn't eat breakfast. She's hungry, but Joe's hungrier because he didn't eat breakfast or lunch!

6. Joan got to work earlier today than yesterday, because she got up earlier.

*Cassette users can have students listen to the script on the tape.

B. Write the sentences in the correct order.

1. Have students write the scrambled words in order.

Answers:
1. She is hungrier than I am.

2. She is poorer today than she was yesterday.

3. I was taller five years ago than I am today.

4. I am older than they are.

5. You are cuter than you think you are.

6. We are happier than ever before.

2. Go over the answers. If students can arrange words in a different, acceptable way, that's okay, too: e.g., Five years ago, I was taller than I am today, etc.

Page 69

C. Change the statements above to questions.

1. Go over directions. Write sentence #1 on the board and make it into a question as an example.

2. Have individuals write the questions. If necessary, have pairs help each other.

3. Have volunteers read their questions for the class.

4. Have pairs check each other's work. Circulate to help as needed.

D. Answer the puzzle below.

This is an optional activity that can also be used as an exercise for fast students who need additional tasks.

36

Delta's Apple Pie, Teacher's Guide 2B

Day Care

Communication Objectives:
>   Plan for child care
>   Read the Yellow Pages

New Structures:
>   Comparative adjectives: irregular *-er* forms

Visuals:

V51	Infant and babysitter at home
V52	Toddler in preschool
V53	4–year–old boy in day care center
V54	6–year–old girl at elementary school
V55	Let's Talk: Who's Going to Take Care of Amy?

Page 70

Review: Older and Younger

1. Students will talk about their families in two steps:
    A. Demonstrate a conversation with a volunteer by asking him how old his (brother or son) is.

    B. Tell the class that your brother or son is older or younger. Give your relative's age (as shown in text).

2. Read the example to students. Have them practice.

3. Have students make up their own comparisons, working in pairs.

Something New: Day Care

1. Briefly explain lesson objectives: To make plans for child care.

2. Show V51–V54 and tell the stories in the text while students listen.

3. Model the sentences and have students repeat.

4. Show each visual and ask questions with "Where…" for class, then individuals, to answer.

☛ **Practice Activity: A Good Place for Bobby**

1. Tell class Bobby is six months old and his parents work. Indicating the visuals, ask which day care is a good place for him. (There may be more than one correct answer.)

2. Ask students to write their answers in the blanks and then discuss their answers with their group (or vice versa).

3. Check work as a class having four different groups each contribute an answer. Have them explain why they chose their answers.

☛ **Practice Activity: Finding Day Care**

1. Ask class how to find a good day care center. Help students think about the Yellow Pages, driving/walking in neighborhood, asking friends, community centers, hospitals, elementary schools, etc. You might want to list ideas on the chalkboard.

2. Have individuals write sentences for several of the ideas.

  Let's Talk: Who's Going to Take Care of Amy?*

1. Use the dialogue visual to establish the context of the conversation.

2. Model the dialogue as students listen, indicating the speakers by pointing to the visual or other means.

3. Model the dialogue again and ask comprehension questions.

4. Model the dialogue and have class repeat.

5. Take one role and have class take other role; then change roles.

6. Divide class in half and have them take the two roles; then have them switch roles.

7. Have volunteers say the dialogue for the class.

 8. Have class open books and practice the dialogue in pairs.

*Cassette users can have students listen to the dialogue first with books closed.

★ **Something Extra:** From the Yellow Pages

Read and/or have students read the four excerpts from the Yellow Pages asking comprehension, then comparison questions after each one.

☞ Practice: "Betty's is better"

1. Look at the ads in the Something Extra section and model sentences with *better, worse,* and *farther.*

2. Have students read the Practice in pairs.

3. Have students make up similar conversations about day care in their own neighborhoods.

✎ Writing

1. Have students read the sentences and fill in the blanks on their own.

2. Check answers by having volunteers read the sentences. Write the comparative forms on the board or on a transparency of the exercise.

📼 Reading: Working Parents*

1. Have students read silently or read the story aloud to them.

2. Ask comprehension questions and then have students read the story again.

3. Initiate discussion by asking whole class and/or individuals the questions on page 75. (Ask students not to write yet.)

*Cassette users can have students listen to the Reading first with books closed.

Discussion

1. Have students discuss in pairs. Ask them not to write anything yet.

2. Ask a volunteer from each pair to give an answer to the whole class.

✎ Writing

1. Have students write their answers to the Discussion questions.

2. Using the board or an overhead transparency, ask different students to write their answers. Have class correct if necessary.

Page 76 🔲 ***A. Suyun had a bad morning. Listen to her tell her friend at work what happened.****

1. Go over the questions for understanding.

2. Have students listen to the dialogue as many times as necessary and write in answers. More advanced students will be able to write complete sentences. Others will write one or two word answers.

3. Choose volunteers to share their answers. This may lead to an optional discussion on the "terrible two's."

Script:

Friend: Hi, Suyun, you look terrible! You look like you've been through World War III.

Suyun: World War III?

Friend: Yes. You look terrible—so worried and tired. What happened?

Suyun My son had a tantrum this morning.

Friend: A tantrum? You mean kicking and crying?

Suyun: Exactly.

Friend: Why?

Suyun: You're not going to believe me.

Friend: Tell me.

Suyun He wanted to wear three jackets to day care and I said, "No."

Friend: Oh, he's two years old?

Suyun: Yes! How did you know?

Friend: I have three big children now, but they were two years old a long time ago. I know it's difficult to have a two–year–old.

Suyun:	I feel so bad in the morning when he cries and then I have to leave him.
Friend:	I know, I know. But you will live through this difficult age. I'll take you to lunch. We'll talk about the terrible two's!
Suyun:	Thank you. You're so nice.
Friend:	Now, don't you cry.

*Cassette users can have students listen to the script on the tape.

B. Check the correct space, write your answers, and discuss your answers with a partner.

Students do this as individuals. Explain that they need to read the questions, check an answer under the "Yes" or "No" column, and then complete the sentences.

Page 77

C. Partner 1 look at this page. Partner 2 look at page 79.

Explain that Mario and Dennis are two fathers at a meeting at a cooperative preschool. They are each going to take notes at the meeting. Partner 1 is going to diccuss his/her notes with Partner 2 and vice versa. Read the story as a class. Check vocabulary. Have pairs tell each other the points they have in their notes.

Page 78

D. Interview your partner.

1. Go over directions. Read questions as a class.

2. Have partners interview each other and then write each other's answers.

3. Have a few volunteers write their sentences on the board. Correct them as a class.

E. Here's what one parent wrote about a cooperative preschool.

Do activity using the vocabulary words in the box. Can be a whole class or individual activity.

Page 79

F. Partner 2 look at this page. Partner 1 look at page 77.

See C above.

Lesson 33

A Better Apartment

Communication Objectives:
> Compare housing
> Read housing ads

New Structures:
> Comparative adjectives with *more*

Visuals:
> V56   mid–size apartment house, Green Street
> V57   larger apartment house, Parkway
> V58   Let's Talk: It's Just a Little More Expensive

Page 80

✔ Review: Child Care

1. Ask what choices parents have for day care, eliciting the types of child care discussed in the previous lesson.

2. Ask students to compare a babysitter to a preschool, etc.

Something New: I Like This One

1. Briefly explain lesson objectives: To compare housing.

2. Show V56–V57 and compare the apartments while students listen.

3. Model the sentences and have students repeat.

Page 81

☛ Practice: "Which one?"

1. Show the first visual and ask questions with "Which one…?" to generate comparative statements about both buildings.

2. Have volunteers form questions about the pictures for class to answer.

3. Have students open books and read individually and/or in pairs what has been practiced orally in the Something New and Practice sections.

▣ Let's Talk: It's Just a Little More Expensive*

1. Use the dialogue visual to establish the context of the conversation.

2. Model the dialogue as students listen, indicating the speakers by pointing to the visual or other means.

3. Model the dialogue again and ask comprehension questions.

4. Model the dialogue and have class repeat.

5. Take one role and have class take other role; then change roles.

6. Divide class in half and have them take the two roles; than have them switch roles.

7. Have volunteers say the dialogue for the class.

 8. Have class open books and practice the dialogue in pairs.

*Cassette users can have students listen to the dialogue first with books closed.

Page 82

☛ Practice: "I want to move"

1. Ask class, "Who wants to move?" After a volunteer answers, ask why he/she wants to move. For example, "Is your apartment too small?" Ask what kind of apartment he/she wants: a bigger apartment, etc.

 2. Have class open books and read the Practice in pairs.

★ Something New: Choosing a Place to Live

1. Read the ads aloud as students listen and follow in their books.

2. Ask "What does _____ mean?" using the spelling of each abbreviation. Have students say the full meaning of each by consulting the list below.

Page 83

☛ Practice: Abbreviations

1. For #1, direct students to write the word next to its abbreviation. You might want students to cover the Something New section on page 82 so they can't refer to it.

2. Have students uncover the words on page 82 and check their answers, including spelling.

3. For #2, tell about your apartment. Write a classified ad for it on the chalkboard beginning with the city and using the abbreviations.

4. Have students each write a classified ad for their own apartments or one they invent. Have them use abbreviations.

5. For #3, have partners switch papers and try to read their partners' ads back to them.

☛ Practice Activity: A Newspaper Ad

1. Ask students to look in the classified section of the newspaper for an apartment for rent ad and bring it to class.

2. Challenge them to guess the meanings of abbreviations they find in the ads.

Page 84 ▦ **Reading:** Do You Want to Own Your Own Home?*

1. Have students read silently or read the story aloud to them.

2. Ask comprehension questions and then have students read the story again.

3. Initiate discussion by asking whole class and/or individuals the questions in the Discussion section.

4. Have pairs or groups continue the discussion on their own.

*Cassette users can have students listen to the Reading first with books closed.

Page 85 ✍ **Writing**

1. Read question #1 and elicit a specific response to the question. Use that answer as a sentence for dictation.

2. Direct students to write the answer as you say it.

3. Repeat steps 1 and 2 to create a dictation for each blank.

4. After the four sentences, you might want to have a volunteer write each answer on the board or an overhead transparency to check for accuracy.

Page 86 **A. Listen to the people tell about the apartments they want. Number the pictures to match what each person wants.***

    1. Go over the directions. Discuss pictures and spaces. Instruct students to listen to the tape and write the number of the speaker under each picture.

    2. Play the tape or read the script.

Script:

1. Linda doesn't have a car. She needs to live close to public transportation. She wants to live near the bus.

2. Phyllis wants her kids to be able to play outside. She is dreaming about having a place with a yard so her children can run, yell, and get dirty.

3. Carey's got a brand new car. He needs a place with a garage. Plus, there are a lot of thefts these days. He wants his car safe, clean, and inside.

4. Layne wants a larger apartment. She works at home and needs a room for all her business stuff. You know what else? She and her husband are about to have a baby, and they only have a studio apartment. Help! She's got to find more room.

5. Bryce wants a view of the ocean. He doesn't care about how many rooms he has. He doesn't care about location. He just wants to see something beautiful when he looks out the window.

*Cassette users can have students listen to the script on the tape.

Page 87 **B. Read.**

Have students read individually and circle any vocabulary words they don't know. Explain vocabulary. Read as a class or have partners read to each other. Guide students to the answer at the bottom of the page.

C. Discuss with your partner.

Partner 1 can read three questions; Partner 2 can read three. They discuss as they go along.

D. Write your answers to questions 5 and 6 above.

Have students write down what they would like in a dream house after they have discussed it with a partner in Exercise C.

Page 89  *I. Listening Comprehension**

    1. Go over the directions for Part I with students.

    2. Read each item of the script two times, at normal conversational speed.

        Script:
        1. Jamal is older than his sister Kanisha. He's 10.

        2. David is younger than his sister Lucia. He's eight.

        3. Bob is taller than his brother Steve.

        4. Jane's apartment is more expensive.

        5. I think that apartment is worse.

        6. She's hungrier than I am.

        7. She's old enough to get a senior citizen discount.

        8. We need a babysitter.

    *Cassette users can have students listen to the script on the tape.

Page 90   *II. Reading and III. Writing*

    1. Go over the directions for Parts II and III with students.

    2. Have class do these sections independently.

    Evaluation Check

    1. Correct evaluation by having student volunteers write their answers on the board or an overhead transparency.

    2. Have class check their answers.

    3. Circulate to make sure students have checked their work accurately.

It's the Nicest One

Communication Objectives:
Compare three or more items
Select furniture
Discuss buying on credit
Fill out a Change of Address form

New Structures:
Superlative adjectives

Visuals:
V59   This is a nice sofa.
V60   This one is nicer than the other.
V61   This sofa is the nicest of all.
V62   Let's Talk: It's the Nicest One in the Store
V63   Let's Talk: Can I Buy It on Credit?

Page 92
✔ Review: Comparing Apartments

1. Read want ads as students follow along.

2. Ask volunteers to compare the two apartments using the vocabulary. To get students started, model: "The three–bedroom apartment is more expensive than the two–bedroom apartment."

3. If students brought in classified ads, you might want to do the Practice Activity from Lesson 33 at this time. (See page 44.)

Page 93
Something New: Nice, Nicer Than, the Nicest

1. Briefly explain lesson objectives: To continue to compare things.

2. Show V59–V61 and describe the sofas while students listen.

3. Model the sentences and have students repeat.

4. Show each visual and make open–ended statements with "This is…" for class, then individuals, to complete.

5. Have students open books and look at the pictures. Read the sentences aloud as they follow along.

☞ Practice: "Which room is the biggest?"

Have students read the Practice in pairs.

Page 94 **Let's Talk:** It's the Nicest One in the Store*

1. Use the dialogue visual to establish the context of the conversation.

2. Model the dialogue as students listen, indicating the speakers by pointing to the visual or other means.

3. Model the dialogue again and ask comprehension questions.

4. Model the dialogue and have class repeat.

5. Take one role and have class take other role; then change roles.

6. Divide class in half and have them take the two roles; then have them switch roles.

7. Have volunteers say the dialogue for the class.

 8. Have class open books and practice the dialogue in pairs.

Page 95 **☞ Practice: "This lamp is the prettiest"**

1. Instruct students to look at the four sets of illustrations.

2. Read the sentences for the first one. Have students repeat.

3. Do the same for the second, third and fourth pictures, asking class to complete the sentences aloud.

Page 96 **Let's Talk:** Can I Buy It on Credit?*

1. Show the visual to establish the context of the conversation.

2. Follow the procedure given in the Let's Talk section above for presenting the dialogue.

 3. Have the students practice in pairs.

*Cassette users can have students listen to the dialogue first with books closed.

☛ Practice: "You need to pay cash"

1. Ask class if you can buy a few different things on credit so that some answers are "yes" and some "no."

2. Model conversations. Have students read and practice in pairs.

3. Faster students can make up and practice their own conversations.

4. You might ask for volunteers to read their dialogues to the class.

Page 97 📼 **Reading:** Cash or Credit*

1. Have students read silently or read the story aloud to them.

2. Ask comprehension questions and then have students read the story again.

*Cassette users can have students listen to the Reading first with books closed.

Discussion

1. Initiate discussion by asking whole class and/or individuals the questions.

2. Have students continue the discussion in pairs or groups.

Page 98

★ Something Extra: Change of Address Form

1. Have students read silently or read the story aloud to them.

2. Ask comprehension questions and then have students read the story again.

✍ Writing

1. Prepare an overhead transparency of the Change of Address form on page 99.

2. Point to headings as you read them to class.

3. Read directions on page 98 as you fill in each section of the form. Use your own address, school address, or a made–up address to fill out the "old address" section. Discuss problem areas such as skipping too many spaces between names, not starting in the first space provided, etc. as you go.

4. Have students open their books to page 98 and read the directions as you read them again aloud.

5. (Optional) You may want to fill out the blank form on the transparency again with some errors students will spot and correct.

6. Direct students to look at the postcard at the top of page 99. Explain that the Kims must write this new address on their Change of Address form.

7. Have students fill in the Kims' new address as directed in #1.

8. Circulate to check their work.

9. Go over the directions for #2. Have students use their own "old" address and fill out the Change of Address form for a move to the new address given.

10. Circulate to check their work.

Lesson 34 Activity Page

Page 101 📼 **A. Listen to the information and fill in the Change of Address form.***

1. Go over directions. Go over form noting spaces for dates. Review how to write dates with two digits each.

2. Play tape or read the script. Pause between items to allow time for writing, or read or play whole script at natural speed more than once.

> **Script:**
> Jaime has to move. He has to fill out a Change of Address form.
> But Jaime has a problem. He broke his arm and he can't write.
> Listen to him give his information and write it on the form.
>
> My last name is Santos. S–A–N–T–O–S.
> My first name is Jaime. J–A–I–M–E.
> My address if fifty nine sixteen Mark Place. That's M–A–R–K. Put P–L for Place.
> The city is Oakland, O–A–K–L–A–N–D, California.
> C–A for California.
> The zip is nine four six one eight.
> Now, the effective date is March thirtieth, nineteen ninety–five.
> Please sign my name under signature. I will try to initial it.
> Thanks for your help.

*Cassette users can have students listen to the script on the tape.

B. Ask two people the questions below. Write their answers in one word.

    1. Go over directions.

    2. Have students move around the room to ask the questions.

    3. If you want, you can extend this activity by making a grid on the board and having volunteers contribute their items.

C. On your own paper, write sentences with the information from B.

    1. Write the example sentence on the board. Elicit several students' information as examples.

    2. Have students write four sentences on their own papers.

    3. Circulate to check their work, or have pairs switch papers and check each other's work.

Lesson 35

Will Our Apartment Be Ready?

Communication Objectives:
> Plan a move
> Request/cancel utility service

New Structures:
> Contrast of *will* and *be going to*

Visuals:
> V64   Moving Is a Lot of Work
> V65   Let's Talk: Will Our Apartment Be Ready?
> V66   Let's Talk: I Think I'm Going to Play Soccer

Page 102

✔ Review: Cash or Charge?

1. Initiate a conversation with a student to model a purchase: e.g., "How much is that dictionary…?" "May I charge it?" etc.

2. Model examples in book.

3. Have students practice.

4. Have pairs make up their own conversations.

Something New: Moving Is a Lot of Work

1. Briefly explain lesson objectives.

2. Show V64 and tell the story in the text while students listen.

3. Ask comprehension questions with *be going to* for class, then individuals, to answer.

4. Have students open books and read the story.

Page 103

☛ Practice: "They're going to rent a truck"

Have students read the Practice in pairs. They can continue with other questions about the story.

Let's Talk: Will Our Apartment Be Ready?*

1. Use the dialogue visual to establish the context of the conversation: Don Kim is talking to the manager/superintendent of his new apartment.

2. Model the dialogue as students listen, indicating the speakers by pointing to the visual or other means.

3. Model the dialogue again and ask comprehension questions.

4. Model the dialogue and have class repeat.

5. Take one role and have class take other role; then change roles.

6. Divide class in half and have them take the two roles; then have them switch roles.

7. Have volunteers say the dialogue for the class.

 8. Have class open books and practice the dialogue in pairs.

*Cassette users can have students listen to the dialogue first with books closed.

Page 104
☛ Practice: "It will be ready on June 1st"

1. Lead a discussion about what the Kims need to do before they move into their new apartment.

 2. Have class open books and read the Practice in pairs.

Page 105
★ Something New: What Are You Going to Do on Saturday?

1. Use the illustrations in the text to practice the *be going to* future.

2. Tell students your plans for after school or the weekend, using "I'm going to…"

3. Ask a student what he/she's going to do and a different student what the first student is going to do to practice the form for *he* and *she*.

4. Model the question, "What are you going to do on Saturday?"

5. Have pairs of students ask each other what they are going to do.

6. Have individuals tell the class what his/her partner is going to do this weekend.

☞ Practice: "I'm going to study"

Have students read the conversations in pairs.

Page 106 **Let's Talk:** I Think I'm Going to Play Soccer

1. Use the dialogue visual to establish the context of the conversation.

2. Model the dialogue as students listen, indicating the speakers by pointing to the visual or other means.

3. Model the dialogue again and ask comprehension questions.

4. Model the dialogue and have class repeat.

5. Have class open books and practice the dialogue in pairs.

6. Explain that when Jim asks "What are you going to do this weekend?", he is using the *be going to* future because he's talking about making plans. When he says "Yes, I will. I promise I'll call you" he is using the *will* future because he's making a promise.
   Note: The choice of future form depends on the situation: *be going to* for making plans; *will* for promising, confirming, or agreeing to do something. In other situations, the forms are interchangeable.

Page 107 **Reading:** Raj and Indira Sidhu*

1. Have students read silently or read the story aloud to them.

2. Ask comprehension questions and then have students read the story again.

3. Initiate discussion by asking whole class and/or individuals the questions.

4. Have students continue the discussion in pairs or groups.

*Cassette users can have students listen to the Reading first with books closed.

✐ Writing

1. Students can be led from the discussion about Raj and Indira's family to what students in the class do with their children when they move.

2. Ask for an answer from a number of volunteers. Write one on the board.

3. Check student work by having individuals read their answers or by teacher observation.

Lesson 35 Activity Pages

Page 108 **A. Listen to the story about Jack and Gloria on their moving day.***

    1. Go over directions. Explain the grid. Students will check the correct space on the grid.

    2. Play the tape or read the script. Repeat whole script as necessary.

        Script:
- My friends Jack and Gloria were planning their move. They were trying to decide who was going to do what.
- Jack said he was going to call to have the electricity turned on in their new apartment.
- Gloria said she was going to call to have the electricity turned off in their old apartment.
- They planned to move on October 31.
- Jack and Gloria made their calls.
- At eight o'clock in the evening, on October thirty–first, the lights went out in their old apartment. Jack tripped, fell down and dropped a box of Gloria's things. He couldn't see with the electricity turned off.
- At the same time, on the same evening, Gloria was shivering and sneezing in their new apartment. She was sure she was going to catch a cold because the electricity wasn't on yet and she was very cold.
- Both Jack and Gloria were angry with each other.
- One had the power turned off too soon. The other had the power turned on too late.

    *Cassette users can have students listen to the script on the tape.

B. Answer the questions below.

    1. Students work in pairs. First they interview each other; then individuals write their own answers.

    2. Volunteers can tell the whole class their stories.

C. Partner 1 look at this page. Partner 2 look at E on page 109.

    Go over directions with class. Examine grid. Remind Partner 1 that his/her grid is on the next page. Practice the example questions first, then have students do the activity in pairs.

Page 109 **D. Ask and answer questions with your classmates.**

     Go over directions and grid to clarify any vocabulary students might need reviewed. Remind class that they must find a different student to sign each space. Practice forming questions with each item: e.g., "Are you going to move this month?" (Timed exercises and prizes make for added excitement.)

E. Partner 2 look at this page. Partner 1 look at C on page 108.

    See C above.

Lesson 36

When Are You Going to Fix It?

Communication Objectives:
> Request repair service
> Complain about household repair problems

New Structures:
> None

Visuals:

V67	a toaster
V68	a coffeemaker
V69	a microwave oven
V70	an iron
V71	a refrigerator
V72	a stove
V73	a washing machine
V74	a dryer
V75	Let's Talk: What's Wrong?
V76	A Bathroom in Trouble
V77	Let's Talk: When Are You Going to Fix It?

Page 110

✔ Review: Weekend Plans

1. Tell students a plan you have for your weekend using *going to*.

2. Ask volunteers to state their plans for the coming week or weekend.

3. Introduce the lesson by saying that many people use weekends to do errands, take things to be repaired, etc.

Something New: Household Appliances

1. Briefly explain lesson objectives: To request repair service for household items.

2. Show V67–V74 and say the vocabulary words while students listen.

3. Model the words and have students repeat.

4. Show each visual and ask questions with "Is this…?" and then "What's this…?" for class, then individuals, to answer.

Page 111 **Let's Talk:** What's Wrong?*

 1. Use the dialogue visual to establish the context: Jae Kim is calling for service on her washing machine.

2. Read the introductory paragraph describing the visual, pointing to the items in the illustration as appropriate.

3. Model the dialogue as students listen, indicating the speakers by pointing to the visual or other means.

4. Model the dialogue again and ask comprehension questions.

5. Model the dialogue and have class repeat.

6. Take one role and have class take other role; then change roles.

7. Divide class in half and have them take the two roles; then have them switch roles.

8. Have volunteers say the dialogue for the class.

 9. Have class open books and practice the dialogue in pairs.

Page 112 ☛ **Practice: "What's wrong with your stove?"**

 1. Show V67–V74 again and ask questions with "What's wrong?" "What's the matter?" etc., so students can offer vocabulary they know for appliances that don't work.

 2. Have students open books and read individually and/or in pairs what has been practiced orally.

 Let's Talk: Do You Repair Toasters?*

1. Have students look at the title and illustration to establish the context of the conversation. Explain that this time Jae Kim needs a toaster repaired.

2. Follow the procedure given in the Let's Talk section above for presenting the dialogue.

3. Have students practice in pairs.

4. Have students read the note at the bottom of the page and discuss.

*Cassette users can have students listen to the dialogue first with books closed.

Something New: A Bathroom in Trouble

 Use V76 to teach the vocabulary. Follow the procedure at the beginning of the lesson for teaching Something New.

☛ Practice: "What's wrong?"

Follow the usual procedure for teaching the Practice.

Let's Talk: When Are You Going to Fix It?*

 Use V77 and follow the usual procedure for teaching Let's Talk.

*Cassette users can have students listen to the dialogue first with books closed.

☛ Practice: "I'm going to fix it tomorrow"

Follow the usual procedure for teaching the Practice. If students ask about the future form used here, explain that the manager is pretending/implying that he has plans to fix the bathroom.

Reading: Tomorrow Never Comes*

Teacher or a strong student can lead a class discussion by giving an answer to question #1, then asking a student question #1, and letting that student and others contribute answers. Teacher corrects sentence construction as appropriate and offers appropriate lifeskills information.

Lesson 36 Activity Pages

  A. Listen and match the problem with the correct room.*

1. Go over the directions. Explain that students will listen only, not look at the illustration for exercise B.

2. Play the tape. Stop it after #1 to show students how the first one is marked. Play the tape as many times as necessary.

Script:
1. The window is still broken in the living room. Can you fix it today, please? It's very cold in here!

2. Excuse me, but my roof is still leaking into the dining room. When are you going to fix it!!?

3. Would you please fix the pipe in the bathroom. It's still leaking. There's a lot of water on the floor!

4. Agggh! Do you hear it? It's dripping again. The faucet in the kitchen!! Just give me your tools and I can fix it myself!

5. Please come right away...the doorknob to the bedroom is broken. Yes, right away! I have to go to work and I'm stuck in the bedroom.

*Cassette users can have students listen to the script on the tape.

B. The manager of Parkview Apartments is going to work in all the apartments this weekend.

Go over directions with students. Suggest partners discuss the building room by room. You may wish to reconvene as a whole class and have volunteers talk about each apartment.

Page 117 **C. Look at the picture on page 116 and answer the questions below.**

Go over directions and example. Have students write complete sentences. Volunteers can write their sentences on the chalkboard.

Unit Twelve Evaluation

Page 119 ### I. Listening Comprehension*

1. Go over the directions for Part I with students.

2. Read each item of the script two times, at normal conversational speed.

   Script:
   1. My faucet drips.

   2. My oven is broken.

   3. I need a Change of Address form.

   4. He's going to pack today.

   5. I want to charge it.

   6. You have to make a down payment.

   7. My apartment is in poor condition.

   8. A man is complaining about his apartment.

*Cassette users can have students listen to the script on the tape.

Page 120 ### II. Reading and III. Writing

1. Go over the directions for Parts II and III with students.

2. Have class do these sections independently.

Evaluation Check

1. Correct evaluation by having student volunteers write their answers on the board or an overhead transparency.

2. Have class check their answers.

3. Circulate to make sure students have checked their work accurately.

Lesson 37

Emergencies and Necessities

Communication Objectives:
Report an emergency
Discuss appropriate times to call 911
Respond to a traffic ticket
Recognize what to do after an auto accident

New Structures:
Modal *must*

Visuals

V78   A house is on fire!
V79   Someone was hurt in an accident!
V80   There's a robbery!
V81   A child is drowning!
V82   Let's Talk: I Need the Paramedics

Other instructional aids: Telephone books from communities your students represent

Page 122

✔ Review: Things that Work and Don't Work

1. Divide class in groups. Have groups select a secretary. Instruct secretary to write the list for the group. When everyone's ready, inform them that they will list everything that leaks. Set the timer. If you have time, have groups now list things that drip.

2. Tell class what you have at home that's in good condition. Have volunteers tell the whole class what they have that's in good condition.

Something New: An Emergency

1. Briefly explain lesson objective: To report an emergency.

2. Use V78–V81, draw on the chalkboard, and explain the sentence given for each visual.

3. Model each sentence while students listen.

4. Post the visuals around the room or place them on the chalk rail and give each one a number. Call out each sentence and have students identify the correct picture by pointing to it or saying the number.

5. Cue with visuals and model, having class and individuals repeat the sentences.

6. Cue with visuals and have class and individual students say the sentences.

7. Have students contribute any discussion they may have about the pictures.

Page 123 ☞ **Practice: "911"**

1. Show pictures on overhead transparency and have students describe what's happening in each picture, or have students open books and talk about each illustration.

2. Model Practice conversations.

3. Have students practice in pairs.

4. Students who finish quickly can ask and answer their own questions.

5. Inventive students can be invited to perform their conversations for the class.

🔲 Let's Talk: I Need the Paramedics*

1. Show the visual to establish the context of the conversation: Jae Kim thinks her father is having a heart attack.

2. Model the dialogue as students listen, indicating the speakers by pointing to the visual or other means.

3. Model the dialogue again.

4. Model the dialogue and have class repeat.

5. Take one role and have class take other role; then change roles.

6. Divide class in half and have them take the two roles; then have them switch roles.

7. Have volunteers say the dialogue for the class.

8. Have class open books and practice the dialogue in pairs.

*Cassette users can have students listen to the dialogue first with books closed.

Page 124 ☞ **Practice: "Was anybody hurt?"**

1. Ask students what emergencies they know about.

2. Look at pictures of emergencies in text. Have students tell what happened.

3. Practice orally as a whole class, in groups, and in pairs; then have class read what they have been practicing orally in pairs.

Page 125

★ Something Extra: Non–emergencies

1. Explain that there are emergencies and non–emergencies. Give personal examples such as you need to get stamps to pay your bills, but you won't die if you don't pay them. Therefore, getting stamps is not an emergency. It's just important, a need.

2. Have students look at the pictures on page 125. Ask someone what happened and if it's an emergency. Explain that it's not. Neither problem is life threatening. (Note: The robbery has already occurred; therefore, it's no longer an emergency.)

☛ Practice Activity: Is this an emergency?

1. Read the explanation of emergencies and non–emergencies to students. Then read the items in the two columns and explain vocabulary. Have students circle the emergencies on their own.

2. Have students check and discuss their answers in pairs.

3. You might ask students if anybody changed their answers after they talked to their partner.

Page 126

☛ Practice Activity: Getting Important Phone Numbers

1. Go over vocabulary with class.

2. Adapt this activity to the phone book in your community. You might want to show where the emergency numbers are found in your students' phone book. Then give each student a copy of the page where the numbers are listed to let them transfer the numbers to the correct spaces in the student book.

★ Something Extra: You *Must* Do Something!

1. Have students look at the illustration.

2. Follow the procedure given in the Let's Talk section on page 62 for presenting the dialogue.

3. Have students practice in pairs.

Delta's Apple Pie, Teacher's Guide 2B   **63**

☞ Practice: "You must pay the fine"

1. Give some examples of things you must do at your school or in your community.

 2. Have students open their books and practice in pairs.

3. Students who finish quickly can make up their own conversations and present them to the class if you wish.

🔊 Reading: What to Do if You Have a Car Accident*

1. Have class read title. Ask a volunteer to explain what it means.

2. Read the selection together as a class and then again in groups or individually.

3. Encourage students to make comments or ask questions about the Reading content.

*Cassette users can have students listen to the Reading first with books closed.

✍ Writing

1. Go over directions with students.

2. Show them how to retrieve the information from the story above. You may want to use an overhead transparency of this page to show how to find the answers in the story.

3. Have students do the Writing independently.

4. Correct as a class.

Page 129 📼 ***A. Check the correct emergency.****

    1. Go over the grid with students. They are to put a check under the correct emergency as they hear each dialogue.

    2. Play the tape or read the script.

> **Script:**
>
> 1. I'm Lois Allen, 849 Nicassio Valley Road. Flames are shooting everywhere! I'm afraid everything will burn. Please send help now!
>
> 2. This is Janet Williams. My father can't breathe. He swallowed the cap of his medicine bottle. Please send someone right away. I don't know what to do!
>
> 3. There's someone trying to break down the door. Now he's kicking it open. Please! This is an emergency! I'm so scared…my name's Renna Brown.

*Cassette users can have students listen to the script on tape.

B. Imagine there's a fire in your apartment.

    1. Go over directions. Explain that each student's answers will be different. If necessary, reiterate that students are writing their most precious items first, least precious last.

    2. Volunteers can share their answers with the class orally. A number of volunteers can write their answers on the board for everyone to read or, in groups, students can read their answers to each other.

    3. Have pairs discuss how their lists are different.

C. Read the story.

    1. Go over these vocabulary words: *freeze, halt, command, shoot, suspect, occur, tragedies.*

    2. Read story to class. Have class read with you.

    3. Ask comprehension questions. Students might remember what happened to the Japanese student who was shot in Louisiana when he went to the wrong address looking for a Halloween party.

    4. Have students discuss in groups. You might want to continue discussion as a class to tell them that while these events are rare, you want them to know the vocabulary so they will be safe.

Home Security

Communication Objectives:
> Identify ways to secure a home
> Ask to borrow something

New Structures:
> Modal *should*

Visuals:
> V83   Lock the doors
> V84   Install a peephole
> V85   Install a deadbolt
> V86   Put a broomstick or dowel...
> V87   Drill a hole for a screw
> V88   Install bars on the windows
> V89   Let's Talk: There Was a Burglary Next Door

Page 130   ✔ **Review:** An Accident

1. Remind students of the word *must*, eliciting examples of things one *must* do.

2. Have students read the introduction as a class.

3. Discuss. Provide information that must be left on the note.

4. Have students work in pairs. Each student must write a note to leave on the car he/she hit. Then students exchange notes and read them.

5. Have volunteers share their notes with the class.

Something New: Home Security

1. Establish the objective of the lesson: To discuss personal safety and home security.

2. Explain the words: *burglar* and *burglary*. (Explain the difference between a burglary and a robbery, which they studied in the previous chapter.)

3. Ask students what they can do to protect their possessions at home. Encourage discussion.

4. Show visuals. Model the sentences for each procedure.

5. Have students identify the procedure as you call it out by pointing to the various visuals.

6. Ask *yes/no* and *either/or* questions about the visuals.

7. Model and have class, groups, individuals repeat.

8. Ask and have class, groups, individuals say the sentences to identify the security procedures.

Page 131 **Let's Talk:** There Was a Burglary Next Door*

1. Show the visual to establish the context of the conversation: Neighbors are talking about a serious problem.

2. Model the dialogue as students listen, indicating the speakers by pointing to the visual or other means.

3. Model the dialogue again.

4. Model the dialogue and have class repeat.

5. Take one role and have class take other role; then change roles.

6. Divide class in half and have them take the two roles; then have them switch roles.

7. Have volunteers say the dialogue for the class.

 8. Have class open books and practice the dialogue in pairs.

*Cassette users can have students listen to the dialogue first with books closed.

Page 132 ☛ **Practice: "I want to secure my apartment"**

1. Talk about what you want to secure your house/apartment. Have volunteers say what they want. Have class practice "I want a…" and "I want to…"

 2. Have students open their books and practice in pairs.

★ **Something Extra:** We Should Do a Lot of Things

1. Explain the objective: To use *should* to give advice.

2. Read the opening paragraph to class. Have whole class/groups/pairs/individuals read.

3. Discuss the illustrations.

4. Have students read sentences under the illustrations.

Page 133

☛ **Practice: "You should keep the door locked"**

1. Give some examples with "We should…" and have students offer more example sentences orally.

2. Have students practice the conversations in the book in pairs.

Page 134

★ **Something Extra:** I Want to Borrow a Drill

1. Explain lesson objective: To use the verbs *borrow* and *lend*.

2. Describe the illustrations. Have students repeat the sentences.

☛ **Practice: "May I borrow your pencil?"**

1. Following the practice above, have students simulate this same conversation using a pencil. Ask for three volunteers to demonstrate the activity before the class.

2. Switch the people so that everyone in the demonstration gets to play each role.

3. In groups of three, have the whole class practice the pencil conversation and change roles as the demonstration group did so that each person will have the opportunity to play each role.

📼 **Reading:** To Feel More Secure*

1. Have students read the story independently.

2. Discuss the story.

3. Have class/groups/individuals read the story.

*Cassette users can have students listen to the Reading first with books closed.

✐ **Writing**

    1. Go over the directions with the students.

    2. Have students fill in the blanks independently.

    3. Check student work by circulating around the room. If you have an overhead transparency prepared, you can have a volunteer fill in the blanks for the class. Students can also write the complete sentences on the chalkboard and check their work from the board.

Lesson 38 Activity Pages

🔊 *A. Imagine you are a police officer and you have to fill out the police report below.* *

    1. Go over the directions with students. Review form indicating that students will fill in the blanks with the correct information they hear from the tape. Practice the kinds of things they might put in the blanks. Inform them that they will need to find the correct space for the information they receive. The information is not given in sequence.

    2. Play the tape or read the script. If students have not completed the forms, repeat the whole script from the beginning as many times as necessary.

Script:

Officer: Hello, I'm Sergeant Marks. Are you Ida Stark?

Ida: Yes.

Officer: May I come in?

Ida: Please do.

Officer: You had a burglary?

Ida: Yes. Somebody broke in. I know it was after one because I was home for lunch and I left at one o'clock.

Officer: What's missing?

Ida: My computer, a string of pearls, my TV, my radio…

Officer: You have any idea who did it?

Ida: No.

Officer: Suspect anybody around here?

Ida:	No.
Officer:	Anything else damaged besides this broken window?
Ida:	I don't think so…What are you doing?
Officer:	I got some nice fingerprints for evidence.
Ida:	Does that mean you'll catch the thief?
Officer:	Keep your fingers crossed. I'll try. You have insurance?
Ida:	Yes.
Officer:	At least that will help some. Doggone it. I left your address in the car. Would you mind telling me your address again?
Ida:	Not at all. It's thirteen forty–one First Avenue, New York, New York, one oh six seven two.
Officer:	Phone number?
Ida:	Three seven eight, two six five one.
Officer:	Thanks a lot.
Ida:	Thank you.

*Cassette users can have students listen to the script on the tape.

Page 137

B. Here's a different story.

1. Read the story aloud to students.

2. Have partners take turns reading the story to each other.

3. Check vocabulary comprehension by asking students what words they don't know and giving them definitions.

4. As a class, talk about what Negesti should do.

5. Have students write their own answers.

6. The teacher can circulate around the room to check answers, student volunteers can write their answers on the chalkboard or partners can check each other.

C. Volunteer to read your story ending to the class.
   Optional.

Page 138   **D. Using the vocabulary words <u>always</u> and <u>never</u>, fill in all the blanks.**
   1. This activity has two parts: Students should fill in the blanks in the right column with *always* and *never*. Then they should draw a line from each problem to its solution.

   2. Encourage students to read both columns first for better understanding. Then have them work in pairs or individually to complete the activity.

Page 139   **E. Mothers are famous for telling children, "You should never..."**
   1. Go over directions. Give a personal example or use the example in the text.

   2. Have students interview each other in pairs.

F. Fill in the blanks with the vocabulary words.
   1. Go over directions with students. Review *borrow* and *lend* by demonstrating with an accessible object such as a student's pencil.

   2. Have students fill in the blanks individually.

   3. Assess by having student volunteers read aloud one sentence each.

Car Troubles

Communication Objectives:
Describe car problems
Request auto service
Speak to a police officer

New Structures:
Modals *could, may, be supposed to*

Visuals:
V90   I'm out of gas.
V91   My battery is dead.
V92   My tire is flat.
V93   My car is overheating.
V94   My windshield is dirty.
V95   Let's Talk: My Car Won't Start
V96   Let's Talk: May I See Your License, Please?

Other instructional aids: A few 8½" by 11" pieces of paper
AAA card or equivalent

Page 140

✔ Review: Home Security

1. Form groups. Have students try to say all six ways they learned to secure a home. Have a secretary for each group write them on a piece of paper as fast as possible. Give a prize or a big round of applause to the group that finishes first.

2. Generate a list of all six ways on the board and review how to do each one.

Something New: Car Problems

1. Explain lesson objective: To identify and describe car problems.

2. Show V90–V94. Explain to students by pointing to the visual or describing what happens when you have this car problem.

3. Model the sentences for the problem and the request for each visual as students listen.

4. Ask *yes/no* and *either/or* questions about the visuals.

5. Model and have class repeat the sentences.

6. Show each visual and have students say the problem and the request.

Page 141 ☛ **Practice: "Could you change it for me?"**

1. Talk about yourself and a flat tire. For example say when and where it happened and whether you fixed it yourself or asked for help with it.

2. Have individual students tell about flat tire experiences.

 3. Have students open their books and read the conversations as a class and in pairs.

4. Practice other requests with *Could you...?*

Page 142 **Let's Talk:** My Car Won't Start*

 1. Show the visual to establish the context of the conversation: A woman can't get her car started.

2. Model the dialogue as students listen, indicating the speakers by pointing to the visual or other means.

3. Model the dialogue again.

4. Model the dialogue and have class repeat.

5. Take one role and have class take other role; then change roles.

6. Divide class in half and have them take the two roles; then have them switch roles.

7. Have volunteers say the dialogue for the class.

 8. Have class open books and practice the dialogue in pairs.

*Cassette users can have students listen to the dialogue first with books closed.

Discussion

1. Show your AAA card or equivalent. Explain what an automobile club is, how much it costs, limits, etc.

2. Go over Discussion questions with whole class.

3. If any students belong to another automobile service club or plan, have the class ask them the Discussion questions.

☛ **Practice Activity: Road Service**

1. Go over directions with students. Model the conversation or have volunteers do it.

2. Have class work in pairs.

3. Watch for a twosome that does it dramatically. Invite the pair to perform for the class.

Let's Talk: May I See Your License, Please?*

1. Show the visual to establish the context of the conversation.

2. Follow the procedure given for presenting the dialogue in the previous Let's Talk section.

 3. Have students practice in pairs.

*Cassette users can have students listen to the dialogue first with books closed.

☛ **Practice: "May I see your registration?"**

1. Explain the meaning of *May I...?*

2. Go over the conversations and then have the students practice in pairs.

☛ **Practice: "That's no excuse"**

1. Explain that students will practice asking what they did wrong, getting the answers and responding, "That's no excuse."

2. Go over the illustrations and vocabulary as a class.

3. Have students practice the conversations in pairs.

🔲 **Reading:** When Your Car Breaks Down*

1. Use the illustration and have students talk about what they think is going on in the picture. Explain the title.

2. Have class read story by themselves.

3. Ask comprehension questions and then have students read the story again.

*Cassette users can have students listen to the Reading first with books closed.

Discussion

1. Go over questions.

2. Lead class discussion or have students work in groups. Volunteers can then give their answers to the whole class.

Page 146
✍ Writing

1. Have students work independently.

2. Correct as a class.

Lesson 39 Activity Pages

Page 147
A. *Find someone for each of the problems below.*
1. Go over directions.

 2. Have students circulate in the class to do this activity.

3. Ask volunteers to read their sentences. Then ask people named in the sentences to elaborate on their stories if they wish, telling them to the whole class.

B. *Read the story.*
1. Read the story to the class. Explain vocabulary words. Tell them not to turn the page to read the answer yet. Read the story as a class or have different volunteers read the story aloud. You can have students read to each other if you prefer.

2. Discuss the story in pairs, groups or as a class. At a certain point have the class turn their books over to read the answer at the bottom of page 48. Read it together or in pairs. Clarify vocabulary. If you wish, ask students how the story makes them feel.

Page 148
C. *Interview your partner. Write his or her answers.*
Read all the questions first. To check answers, have volunteers write answers on the chalkboard. Add or correct information as needed.

Unit Thirteen Evaluation

Page 149 **I. Listening Comprehension***

    1. Go over the directions for Part I with students.

    2. Read each item of the script two times, at normal conversational speed.

        Script:
        1. Call 911.

        2. I think my father is having a heart attack.

        3. Call an ambulance.

        4. You must pay your tickets or we will impound your car.

        5. Put a dowel in the door frame.

        6. May I borrow your drill?

        7. It was a hit–and–run accident.

    *Cassette users can have students listen to the script on the tape.

Page 150 **II. Reading and III. Writing**

    1. Go over the directions for Parts II and III with students.

    2. Have class do these sections independently.

Evaluation Check

    1. Correct evaluation by having student volunteers write their answers on the board or an overhead transparency.

    2. Have class check their answers.

    3. Circulate to make sure students have checked their work accurately.

Lesson 40

Calling In Sick

Communication Objectives:
Call in sick
Discuss sick leave
Express sympathy

New Structures:
None

Visuals:

V97   She has a bad cold.
V98   Sally doesn't feel well today
V99   John is not at work today.
V100   He's calling in sick.
V101   Let's Talk: My Husband Will Be Out Ill Today

Page 152   ## ✔ Review: Car Trouble

1. Have students work with a partner or a group to make up sentences and write them down.

2. Have volunteers read their sentences to the class or write them on the chalkboard.

Something New: Out Ill

1. Explain lesson objective: To report illness to work or school.

2. Ask students if they are or were sick. Elicit the problem.

3. Show the visuals. Read students the sentences, pointing to various parts of the visual as appropriate.

4. Ask *yes/no* and *either/or* questions about the visuals.

5. Model and have class, groups, individuals repeat.

6. Ask and have class, groups, individuals tell you about the pictures.

Page 153 **Let's Talk:** My Husband Will Be Out Ill Today*

 1. Show the dialogue visual to establish the context of the conversation: A woman is calling work for her husband, who is ill.

2. Model the dialogue as students listen, indicating the speakers by pointing to the visual or other means.

3. Model the dialogue again.

4. Model the dialogue and have class repeat.

5. Take one role and have class take the other role; then change roles.

6. Divide class in half and have each half take a role; then switch roles.

7. Have volunteers say the dialogue for the class.

8. Have class open books and practice the dialogue in pairs.

*Cassette users can have students listen to the dialogue first with books closed.

Page 154 ☛ **Practice: "My wife is sick today"**

 1. Tell students they will practice stating the situation and responding.

2. Give an example of what you might have done recently when you were absent.

3. Go over the conversations as a class.

4. Have class open their books and practice the exercises in pairs.

☛ **Practice: "I hope he feels better soon"**

1. Tell students that they are going to practice giving sympathy with "I hope..."

2. Give an example of a real–life situation if appropriate.

3. Follow the same procedure as above.

Page 155 ☛ **Practice Activity: I'm sorry you're sick**

1. Go over directions with class.

2. Go over the sentences.

3. Ask two students to demonstrate the procedure. Then have the second student start a similar conversation with a third student, and on in a chain.

 4. Explain that students will speak to others in their group in a chain. Have them continue for 10 minutes.

★ Something Extra: Calling In Late

1. Ask the class who has a job. Ask this/these person(s) if they are ever late and how they handle it.

2. Read the Something Extra passage to the class as they follow along.

3. Clarify vocabulary. You might want to explain how people get to work or school in different parts of the country or world.

4. Have individuals practice each of the excuses by repeating after you.

5. Have pairs practice giving excuses and saying what time they expect to get to work.

Page 156
☞ Practice: "I'm sorry, I'm going to be late"

1. Have students look at the illustration. Elicit the problem in the picture.

2. Follow the procedure given in the previous Let's Talk section for presenting the dialogue.

3. Have students practice in pairs.

📼 Reading: Sick Leave*

1. Discuss the illustration and explain any information students don't know about time cards.

2. Read story to class or have students read independently.

3. Discuss story, asking comprehension questions.

4. Have students read story again.

*Cassette users can have students listen to the Reading first with books closed.

Page 157
Discussion

1. Go over Discussion questions.

2. Have students discuss in pairs or groups and return with information for whole class.

✍ Writing

1. Discuss the illustration. Ask students what parent must do before child can return to school. (Write a note to the teacher.)

2. Go over the directions.

3. Go over the parts of the note.

4. Read the note with the blanks. Instruct students to fill in the blanks (in pencil if possible).

5. Have volunteers read their letters to the class and/or write the complete letter on the chalkboard or overhead transparency.

Lesson 40 Activity Pages

Page 158 **A. Listen to Ms. Jones, a teacher, take attendance in her class.***

1. Go over directions with class. Clarify vocabulary—present, absent, tardy. You might orient students by telling them that you take attendance and showing them the materials you use. Then go over the grid, making sure they understand that P stands for present, etc. Tell students that they will be given the information in order. They will hear Worknesh's name first and so on.

2. Play the tape or read the script.

   Script:
   Teacher: Worknesh?

   Student: Present.

   Teacher: Hung Ha?

   Student: Here.

   Teacher: Susan?

   Student: Here.

   Teacher: Tekle…You were late…That's a tardy.

   Student: Here.

   Teacher: Nikolay…Nikolay?

Student: He's absent.

Teacher: Maria Elena…You were tardy.

Student: Here. I'm sorry I was late.

Teacher: Juan?

Student: Here.

Teacher: Jacques?

Student: He had a doctor's appointment, remember?

Teacher: Thanks…Jean Marie?

Student: She's absent.

Teacher: Rony?

Student: Present.

Teacher: Melinda?

Student: Present.

Teacher: Sonia…Where is she?

Student: Here!

*Cassette users can have students listen to the script on the tape.

B. Read this with your partner or as a group.
Students first read, write their answers, and then discuss. You may want to extend the discussion to talk about your class.

Page 159
C. Fill in the blanks with the vocabulary words.
1. Point out that some answers are two–word answers, some are one–word answers. Each vocabulary selection is used only once.

2. Encourage students to read their completed stories to themselves two or three times to check their answers in the context of the whole story.

A Good Employee

Communication Objectives:
Ask for help at work
Discuss qualities in good employees
Read pay checks

New Structures:
Adverbs

Visuals:

V102   She's a quick worker.
V103   He's a careful driver.
V104   He's a neat painter.
V105   She's a polite waitress.
V106   His English is good.
V107   She's a fast typist.
V108   Let's Talk: How's Mrs. Green Doing?

Page 160

✔ Review: Calling In Sick

1. Remind students how to call in sick.

2. Break students into groups. Instruct them to compose a conversation. Have one student be the secretary. Everyone participate in writing the conversation (without looking in the book), and two act out the conversation for the class.

3. If you wish, have groups exchange conversations so that one group is acting out the conversation another group has written.

Something New: She Works Quickly

1. Explain lesson objective: To talk about how people work.

2. You might want to talk very quickly and then tell what you have done by saying, "I talked quickly," etc.

3. Use V102–V107 and identify the various activities, modeling the two sentences for each as students listen.

4. Have students identify the activities by pointing to them as you name them.

5. Ask *yes/no* and *either/or* questions about the workers.

6. Model and have class, groups, individuals repeat.

7. Have students describe the workers and how they work as you show the visuals.

Page 162 **Let's Talk:** How's Mrs. Green Doing?*

1. Show the visual to establish the context of the conversation: Mrs. Green is new on the job and her supervisor wants to know if she's doing well.

2. Model the dialogue as students listen, indicating the speakers by pointing to the visual or other means.

3. Model the dialogue again.

4. Model the dialogue and have class repeat.

5. Take one role and have class take other role; then change roles.

6. Divide class in half and have each half take a role; then change roles.

7. Have volunteers say the dialogue for the class.

 8. Have class open books and practice the dialogue in pairs.

*Cassette users can have students listen to the dialogue first with books closed.

Discussion

1. Go over questions with class.

2. Have students work in groups asking and answering questions.

3. Circulate to make sure students are engaged in communicating with each other.

★ **Something Extra:** Can You Show Me This Again?

1. To communicate the meaning of this interaction, you might want to pick some work task, such as sewing on a button by machine in a factory. Explain it and act it out for students showing, at some point, that you are confused and don't know what to do.

2. Using the previous example and others, such as getting stumped when filling out a form, or learning to drive, etc., model the language in Part A saying what the problem is. Have students repeat.

3. Go to Part B, and using the language from Part A, add a question from Part B to go with it. Ask volunteers to demonstrate the same thing.

4. Break students into pairs. Have them string a sentence from Part A and one from Part B together.

5. To follow up, ask in what other situations students might use the language they've just learned.

Page 163 ☛ **Practice: "She writes neatly"**

1. Go over the conversations with the class.

2. Have students practice in pairs.

Page 164 **Reading:** Pay Checks*

1. Explain to students that pay checks have these items on them. Go over the list with them.

2. Clarify the vocabulary.

3. Have students look at the bottom of the page to read explanations of items on the check.

4. Have partners ask each other the meanings of the terms on the list.

5. If students still have questions, you may want to extend this Reading into a class discussion.

*Cassette users can have students listen to the Reading first with books closed.

Page 165 ***A. Listen to the conversation between Jorge and his boss.****

    1. Go over directions with students. Read the form with them. Make sure they understand what is on the chart and the meaning of the vocabulary.

    2. Inform students that they are to put a check in the correct space. They will need to listen for the vocabulary on the form and other clue words such as synonyms. For example, you might call their attention to #2 on the form and ask for another way to say "works quickly." Someone will offer "works fast." (Note: The reviewer on the tape will go down the form from top to bottom, so students won't have to hunt through the form to fill it in.)

    3. Play the tape or read the script. Repeat the whole conversation as many times as necessary.

        Script:

        Boss: Jorge, come in. Sit down.

        Jorge: Thank you.

        Boss: Have you ever been reviewed?

        Jorge: No, I haven't.

        Boss: A review is how management tells you how you are doing on the job. There's nothing to be nervous about. All of us at this factory appreciate your good work.

        Jorge: Thank you.

        Boss: But I want to go over this form with you. You received mostly "fives."

        Jorge: Fives?

        Boss: Yes. You see, supervisors evaluate how an employee works on the job by using numbers from one to five. Look at the form. One is very low. Five is very high. See work style, attitude, appearance, punctuality, attendance and finally, the supervisor's comments?

        Jorge: Yes.

Boss:	Number one: Performs duties correctly. I gave you a five, the highest possible score, because you always do your job correctly.
Jorge:	Thank you.
Boss:	On number two, you got a four, another high mark. Number three, you got a three, which is right in the middle, because I think you can write more neatly. You can improve a little here.
Jorge:	Yes, I will.
Boss:	Now, for number four. You got a two for "works safely" because I still don't think you understand. I want you to work more carefully. You must be safe. If you have a bad accident, there won't be anybody sitting here listening to your next evaluation. Do you understand?
Jorge:	Yes.
Boss:	It's very important...Now, for number five, you got a five. Number six, you got a five. You should know that I think number six is the most important thing you can do well on this job. An employee that's helpful won't ever be replaced. On number seven, you got a five 'cause you dress fine. On number eight, you got a four. (I understand that the bus is not one hundred percent reliable.) And, for number nine, you got a five... Overall? My comments? I am warning you to be safe, but you are a very good employee. I am recommending that you get a raise.
Jorge:	A raise is all right with me. Thank you, sir. I appreciate that. And I won't take any more chances. I promise, I'll work safely. I won't climb on any more boxes.

*Cassette users can have students listen to the script on the tape.

B. Look at the performance review form on page 165.

Page 166
Tell students to check or circle the three most important attributes about an employee and discuss them with a partner. Encourage them to tell why, including giving examples from their own work experience.

C. Partner 1 look at this page. Partner 2 look at F on page 167.
    1. Go over the example question.

    2. Have students ask and answer questions about the missing information.

D. Henrietta Jones wants her employees to be more positive.
    1. Ask students if they know people who are negative and people who are positive. Give examples.

    2. Go over the negative example and the rewritten positive example.

    3. Have students work independently or in pairs. Pairs can correct each other or volunteers may write their signs on the board. Artistic students can be encouraged to make beautiful signs.

Page 167
E. Read this story and discuss the questions below.
    1. This is the story of an actual job situation. The names have been changed. Read as a class, in pairs, or as individuals.

    2. Explain vocabulary. You might want to discuss the different jobs in a restaurant.

    3. Have students write their answers before they read the answer at the bottom of the page. You can ask volunteers to read their answers to the class.

    4. Read the answer at the bottom of the page and discuss further if necessary.

F. Partner 2 look at this page. Partner 1 look at C on page 166.
    See C above.

Lesson 42

Following Instructions

Communication Objectives:
> Give directions to a destination
> Ask for clarification
> Follow employers' instructions
> Identify emergency plans

New Structures:
> Object pronouns

Visuals:
> V109   When you go into the A Building...
> V110   Take the elevator...
> V111   When you come out of the elevator...
> V112   Walk toward the lunch room...
> V113   Then you'll see a double door...
> V114   Go through that door...
> V115   Let's Talk: Please Take These Papers to Mr. Simpson's Office

Page 168

✔ Review: Good Workers

1. Make up examples with adverbs by telling students that they are sitting quietly, smiling beautifully, etc.

2. Remind students that they studied ways to talk about how people work. Review what they learned from pages 160–161.

3. Have students form groups to complete the sentences on page 168.

4. Ask volunteers to read their sentences.

Something New: Directions

1. Explain lesson objective: To give and understand directions.

2. Show V109–114 and model the sentence associated with each visual.

3. Go through the procedures of asking questions, having students repeat, and having students say the directions that go with each visual.

☞ Practice: "Where is his office again?"

1. Place V109–V114 on the chalk rail or post them around the room.

2. Model giving the directions to Mr. Simpson's office by saying each step while looking at the pictures.

3. Have a volunteer tell you the directions, and ask clarification questions to get him or her to repeat each step.

4. Model example questions that students can use if they need clarification. Have students repeat.

 5. Instruct pairs to practice giving the directions and then using the example questions to clarify.

▰ Let's Talk: Please Take These Papers to Mr. Simpson's Office*

 1. Show the dialogue visual to establish the context of the conversation: A woman in an office is asking a man to deliver some papers to someone else at work.

2. Model the dialogue as students listen, indicating the speakers by pointing to the visual or other means.

3. Model the dialogue again.

4. Model the dialogue and have class repeat.

5. Take one role and have class take other role; then change roles.

6. Divide class in half and have each half take a role; then switch roles.

7. Have volunteers say the dialogue for the class.

 8. Have class open books and practice the dialogue in pairs.

*Cassette users can have students listen to the dialogue first with books closed.

☞ Practice: "You can give her the papers"

1. Explain to students that they are about to practice different kinds of instructions people use at work.

2. Discuss illustrations to orient students. Demonstrate as appropriate.

3. Model the conversations and have students repeat.

4. Have students practice the conversations in pairs.

5. Circulate to make sure students are practicing.

Page 171 ✑ **Writing**

1. Go over instructions with class.

2. Have students complete the Writing section independently or in pairs.

3. Have volunteers read the completed sentences and/or write them on an overhead transparency or the chalkboard.

Page 172 🔘 **Reading:** In Case of Fire*

1. Use the illustration to establish context and for pre–reading predictions.

2. Read the sign as a whole class, but have individuals read the story by themselves.

3. Ask comprehension questions and then have students read the story again.

*Cassette users can have students listen to the Reading first with books closed.

Discussion

1. Go over Discussion questions with class.

2. Have students discuss the questions in groups.

3. Resume discussion with whole class. (You might want to be prepared with the details for your school site before you convene for a class discussion.)

Page 173 **A. Fill in the blanks with the correct words.**

Go over directions with students making sure they fill in the correct pronoun first and then draw a line from the situation on the left to the matching sentence on the right.

Page 174 **B. Find the Personnel Office.**

1. Go over directions and discuss floor plan (which can be copied and made into an overhead transparency). Explain that one partner will need to get to the second floor by elevator; the other partner will get to the second floor by stairs. Review expressions they can use.

2. Have pairs prepare for the oral work in exercise C. Partner 1 writes directions for Partner 2 and vice versa.

C. Tell your partner the directions you wrote.

1. Explain that each partner will now give directions to the other. As Partner 1 gives Partner 2 directions, Partner 2 draws his/her path beginning at the stairs. (Partner 1 begins drawing at the elevator.)

2. Have partners check their maps with each other. Volunteer partners can draw their maps on the overhead using different color pens.

Unit Fourteen Evaluation

Page 175 **I. Listening Comprehension***

1. Go over the directions for Part I with students.

2. Read each item of the script two times, at normal conversational speed.

Script:
1. I'm sick today.

2. I hope she feels better tomorrow.

3. John is out ill today.

4. I'm sorry I'm going to be late.

5. He learns quickly and he works carefully.

6. I listen carefully and I practice every day.

7. When you go into the building, you'll see an elevator on your left.

8. Walk toward the lunchroom.

*Cassette users can have students listen to the script on the tape.

Page 176 **II. Reading and III. Writing**

1. Go over the directions for Parts II and III with students.

2. Have class do these sections independently.

Evaluation Check

1. Correct evaluation by having student volunteers write their answers on the board or an overhead transparency.

2. Have class check their answers.

3. Circulate to make sure students have checked their work accurately.

Lesson 43

Applying for a Job

Communication Objectives:
>   Respond to job announcements
>   Talk about work experience
>   Fill out job applications

New Structures:
>   Verb phrase + preposition

Visuals:
>   V116   Help Wanted
>   V117   Let's Talk: I'm Interested in the Job

Page 178

✔ Review: Directions

1. Tell the class you will review directions.

2. Form groups and assign each group the task of giving directions to a location in or around your school. You might want to have a secretary in each group write the directions, too. Volunteers in each group can then give directions to their assigned place.

Something New: Help Wanted

1. Explain lesson objective: To answer an ad for a job.

2. Show the visual and ask class if anyone has ever seen a Help Wanted sign. Discuss as you would a Reading segment, eliciting predictions. Go over the vocabulary on the sign. (Note that the words *waiter/waitress* are gradually being replaced with the non gender–specific term *server*.)

3. Read the story to the class as students listen.

4. Ask comprehension questions. Explain new vocabulary.

5. Have students open books and follow along as you read the story again.

Page 179

☛ Practice Activity: I have experience as a waiter

1. Go over directions with students.

2. Clarify vocabulary words. You may want to ask volunteers to explain the words this time.

3. Have students read the sentences and fill in the blanks.

4. Check student answers by circulating throughout the class, having students read their answers aloud, or having them write the sentences on an overhead transparency or the chalkboard.

Let's Talk: I'm Interested in the Job*

1. Show the visual to establish the context of the conversation: Andre, the fellow looking at the Help Wanted sign, is now calling for a job.

2. Model the dialogue as students listen, indicating the speakers by pointing to the visual or other means.

3. Model the dialogue again.

4. Model the dialogue and have class repeat.

5. Take one role and have class take other role; then change roles.

6. Divide class in half and have each half take a role; then have them switch roles.

7. Have volunteers say the dialogue for the class.

 8. Have class open books and practice the dialogue in pairs.

*Cassette users can have students listen to the dialogue first with books closed.

Page 180 ☛ **Practice: "Hello?"**

1. Tell students they will practice calling about jobs.

2. Go over the ads by using the books, copying the ads on the board, or making an overhead transparency of page 180.

3. Go over the conversations and have volunteer pairs read them. Then have the whole class practice in pairs.

4. Ask students to close their books and continue practicing similar conversations in pairs.

★ **Something Extra:** I'd Like to Fill Out an Application

    1. Discuss newspaper ad with class and explain the phrase *Apply in Person*.

    2. Read about the ad as students listen.

    3. Have students practice the conversation using the job titles they have selected. (You can do this as a chain drill, with students repeating the conversation down each row or around each table or group.)

☛ **Practice: "Do you have any experience?"**

    1. Go over experience section of a job application form asking students if they have ever seen something like this before and having them tell you where.

    2. Explain the context of the dialogue, a job interview, and go over the questions and answers.

    3. Have students practice in pairs.

    4. Follow the same procedure for the References section and conversation.

🔊 **Reading:** Application Forms*

    1. Introduce the Reading by telling students that they will find out how to fill out a job application form.

    2. Start with independent reading.

    3. Read aloud to the class, stopping to stress the points in each paragraph.

    *Cassette users can have students listen to the Reading first with books closed.

Discussion

    1. Guide the discussion, providing vocabulary as needed. Ask follow–up questions to develop job application concepts in more depth if you wish.

    2. Encourage students to collect all the necessary information on one piece of paper that they can take with them when they have to fill out a job application.

✎ **Writing**

    1. Go over directions. Show students how to fill in the grid on the next page.

    2. Have students work independently.

    3. Check student work by circulating around the room.

Lesson 43 Activity Pages

Page 184 **A. Listen to the job announcements.***

   1. Tell students they will hear a list of job openings. Tell them that sometimes jobs are announced on radio, television, and over the phone. These are job announcements from one company as they might hear over the phone. They will listen for the words in each announcement, and write the word or words next to the abbreviation. In the first one, they will have to listen for the word "month" and write it next to "mo.," etc.

   2. As usual, play the tape or read the script as many times as necessary. At the end of the listening activity ask volunteers to write the correct spelling of the words on the chalkboard.

        Script:
        As of Monday, September 10, the following positions are open:

Clerk Typist:	Salary fifteen hundred a month.
Electrician:	Must be Union member. Pay is eleven dollars an hour.
Typist:	Must be able to type sixty words per minute.
Gift Wrapper:	Christmas season only. Part time.
Cashier:	Employee restaurant. Full time.
Personnel Manager:	Experience necessary.
Telemarketing:	Sales. Salary plus commission.
Teacher's Aide:	High school diploma necessary.

        All positions include excellent benefits.

        Comron is a national organization and an equal opportunity employer.

        To hear the job listings again, push the star key on your touchtone phone.

   *Cassette users can have students listen to the script on the tape. The announcement will be repeated after the sound of the star key on the phone.

B. Read the stories.

1. Discuss the pictures. Have students read the two stories as a class, in pairs, or as individuals. Have pairs discuss Liliana's and Pam's dilemmas.

2. Ask students for their ideas. Then, have students turn their books over and read the answers at the bottom of page 185.

Page 185   ### C. How did Liliana get a different job?

1. Have students complete the sentences.

2. Discuss the value of volunteering and gaining non–paid experience, accepting on–the–job training, etc. in building up work experience.

A Job Interview

Communication Objective:
Prepare for a job interview

New Structures:
Linking verbs

Visuals:
V118   Maria called about a job opening.
V119   She filled out an application.
V120   Now she has to go for a job interview.
V121   Let's Talk: I Feel Nervous

Page 186

✔ Review: Work Experience

1. Match students up in an imaginative way so that people who aren't usually partners get to be partners for this exercise: e.g., Form an inner circle and an outer circle, having people in each circle face each other to review work experience.

2. Partners should ask each other if they have any work experience. Instruct them to tell where they worked, what job they had and how long they worked there. Model or have a volunteer team model activity.

Something New: A Job Interview

1. Explain lesson objective: Students will prepare for a job interview.

2. Show visuals. Model the language.

3. Have students identify the activity as you provide the language.

4. Ask *yes/no* and *either/or* questions about the visuals.

5. Model and have class, groups, individuals repeat.

6. Ask and have class, groups, individuals answer to identify visuals.

Page 187 **Let's Talk:** I Feel Nervous*

1. Show the visual to establish the context of the conversation: Maria is talking about her upcoming job interview with her friend Carmen. She's nervous.

2. Model the dialogue as students listen, indicating the speakers by pointing to the visual or other means.

3. Model the dialogue again.

4. Model the dialogue and have class repeat.

5. Take one role and have class take other role; then change roles.

6. Divide class in half and have each half take a role; then switch roles.

7. Have volunteers say the dialogue for the class.

8. Have class open books and practice the dialogue in pairs.

*Cassette users can have students listen to the dialogue first with books closed.

☞ Practice: "What should I say?"

1. Ask students if they talk to their friends or family members about what to say or do on a job interview.

2. Provide them with the language, "What should I say?" "What should I do?"

3. Ask the questions in the Practice and similar questions about behavior, dress, etiquette, etc. for a job interview.

4. Have students open their books and practice conversations in pairs.

5. Volunteers can roleplay a similar conversation: giving a friend advice about a job interview.

Page 188 ## ☞ Practice: Should

1. Go over directions with students. They are to write what they think they should do. You can help them by offering a humorous opposite such as "You should spill coffee" or "You should have chocolate on your shirt," getting a "No" response and then leading them to write what they should do to get ready for a job interview.

2. Have volunteers offer their suggestions and list them on the board if you like.

Page 189

☛ **Practice: "Don't worry"**

1. Ask students how they feel by saying, "You look nervous. What's wrong?" or "You look happy. What happened?" Talk about their responses, saying "_____ looks nervous because…," etc.

2. Have students open their books and read items #1–4 in pairs.

3. When students get to #5–6, have them complete the conversations orally, and then in writing.

4. Volunteers can read their conversations to the class in pairs.

Page 190 **Reading:** Preparing for a Job Interview*

1. Use the illustration and the title to establish context and make predictions about what the Reading will be about.

2. Have class read story by themselves.

3. Ask comprehension questions and then have students read the story again as you read aloud.

*Cassette users can have students listen to the Reading first with books closed.

Discussion

1. Have class work in groups asking and answering questions.

2. You might want to have various groups report back with their answers.

3. After students report the results of their discussion, you might want to let the whole class amplify on what they have said in an extended class discussion.

Page 191 ✍ **Writing**

1. Go over vocabulary words in the box.

2. Have students do this section on their own.

3. Check class work by having students read their sentences aloud to the whole class or in groups. Student volunteers can also write the sentences on the chalkboard or on an overhead transparency.

Lesson 44 Activity Pages

Page 192 **A. Listen to this boss tell what she likes in her employees.***

1. Go over directions with students. Check their comprehension of the items in the grid. Tell them they are going to hear things a boss thinks during an interview, but never tells a job applicant. It's information that can help them be successful at getting jobs.

2. Play the tape or read the script and have students check *should* or *shouldn't* as they listen.

   Script:
   Hello. I'm Susan Dempsey. I run an organization with about 20 employees. I have been a boss for a long time. Let me share some information about how I think you can have a successful job interview.

   1. Be on time. If you are late, you look bad. You're starting off on the wrong foot. First impressions are important.

   2. Sell yourself, but be honest. Don't get a job you can't do. You'll cause problems for everyone—especially yourself.

   3. Know something about the company or organization you want to work for—what it makes, what the people do there.

   4. Listen to the person interviewing you. Don't talk about yourself all the time.

   5. Dress appropriately for the job. Have clean hands. Women shouldn't wear see–through clothes. Bosses want women to look like professionals. They don't want women in party clothes.

   6. Don't come to the interview with a friend. An interview is not a party. You need to look serious.

   7. Talk about your goals. Say what you want in the future. If you want to move up, a boss usually thinks that's good. It looks like you are going to work hard. That makes you look good.

*Cassette users can have students listen to the script on the tape.

B. Read the story and think about all of your skills.

1. Read the story to the class. Partners can then read the story to each other. Check for comprehension. Model the example questions and answers. Ask volunteers to act out the examples.

2. Have students ask and answer questions in pairs. Make it clear that they will talk about their own skills.

3. After students interview each other, have individuals write their own answers at the top of page 193. Check by asking volunteers to tell what they can do and where they did it.

Page 193

C. When you apply for a job, you have to fill out an application form.

1. Before students begin this activity, talk about going to apply for a job and having to fill out an application form. Ask them if they have a problem remembering dates and addresses. Tell them that many people take the information they will need to put on the application form with them because they know they can't remember everything.

2. Read the explanation paragraph to the students. You might also want them to read the paragraph to themselves and/or partners. Go over the directions, "Fill out the form..." Explain the grid. Review the example. Tell them they will write in the job they have now, or their last job, under the example. Explain that job applicants usually write their last job first.

3. Go over the checking exercise with students making sure that it's clear and that they do #1–4. Stress that everything students write should make them look good so that they will get the job.

Lesson 45

I Got the Job!

Communication Objectives:
Answer interview questions
Talk about skills
Discuss job advancement

New Structures:
Contrast of present perfect and past

Visuals:

V122 Have you worked as a carpenter before?
V123 Have you ever been a babysitter before?
V124 Have you ever worked in a restaurant before?
V125 Have you ever worked in the United States before?
V126 Let's Talk: Have You Been a Cashier Before?

Page 194

✔ Review: Should and Shouldn't

1. Tell students they are going to practice using *should* and *shouldn't*.

2. Form groups. Have each group select one person they are going to help prepare for a job interview.

3. The volunteer asks questions and members of the group answer, "Yes, you should" or "No, you shouldn't." Then group members give additional information they think of. A secretary can write the advice and share it with the class, if you like.

Something New: Your Previous Experience

l. Explain lesson objective: To talk about your work skills and experience.

2. Use V122–V125 to show what kind of experience each person has had.

3. Model the conversation as students listen, indicating the speakers.

4. Model the conversation again and have students repeat.

5. Have volunteers say the dialogues for the class.

6. Have class open books and practice the conversations in pairs.

Page 195 **Let's Talk:** Have You Been a Cashier Before?*

 1. Show the dialogue visual to establish the context of the conversation: Joe is applying for a job in a store.

2. Follow the procedure given in Something New for presenting the dialogue.

3. Have the students practice in pairs.

*Cassette users can have students listen to the dialogue first with books closed.

Page 196 ☛ **Practice: "What did you do there?"**

1. Use illustrations to cue practice. Clarify any vocabulary or illustrations such as the personnel agency.

2. Practice as a class and/or in pairs.

Page 197 ★ **Something Extra:** Job Skills

1. Go over the title and give a brief definition of *skills*.

2. Read the passage to the students.

3. Check for comprehension.

4. Have individuals read the passage to themselves.

5. Read the passage again and then ask student volunteers to answer the questions.

6. Have pairs read the conversations and fill in their own skills. Circulate and supply any vocabulary students may need.

7. Have volunteers present their conversations to the class after they have practiced them.

Reading: Moving Up*

1. Getting a job is different in this country than what students may expect. Beginning workers can't usually land high–paying, unskilled jobs in labor any more. They have to start on minimum wage jobs. The purpose of this reading is to help students understand how this process works.

2. Have students do the Reading on their own, or read the passages to them.

3. Ask comprehension questions.

4. Have partners read the passage to each other.

Discussion

1. Go over Discussion questions with class.

2. Have students work in pairs again to ask and answer the questions.

Page 198   ✍ **Writing**

1. Go over directions with students. Explain that they need to read the whole story to be able to fill in the blanks.

2. Have students fill in the blanks independently.

3. Have partners or volunteers from the whole class read the completed story to each other. You can also have a volunteer write the whole story or just the verbs on the board or on an overhead transparency.

Lesson 45 Activity Page

Page 199 🔲 ***A. Listen to the boss tell what he wants an employee to do on the job.****
In this generalized listening activity, students will listen for main ideas.

1. Go over directions with students. Tell them that they are going to hear how a boss wants people to work on the job. Help them understand that they are going to listen for three pieces of advice and write them down.

2. Read the script at normal speed or play the tape as many times as necessary.

> **Script:**
> Hi, I am the manager of many pharmacies. I have seen many employees in my life. I prefer people with no experience because I like to teach them how to do their jobs. I like teaching people to be good employees. Here are three of the most important things I teach:
>
> 1. Help the customer. Customers make our stores. If they don't like us, they will go to a different store. Customers are more important than anything. So, first, help the customer.
>
> 2. Make suggestions to the boss. If you have a good idea, tell the boss. If it's a good idea, it will make the boss look good. The boss will like you and help you. So, second, make good suggestions to the boss. If you know how the store, or factory, or office can work better, make suggestions.

3. Report a problem. For example, if you work in a pharmacy and there is no aspirin on the shelf, think like the boss. Ask yourself, "Where is the aspirin?" Then, you think of it before the boss says, "Is there any aspirin in the back?" If you check for aspirin in the back, you can report the problem better. You can say to the boss, "There isn't any aspirin on the shelf and there isn't any in the back of the store, either." That's reporting a problem.

So help the customer, make suggestions, and report a problem. These three things will make you an excellent employee.

3. Have students discuss their answers with a partner.

4. Discuss the answers with the whole class and elicit examples from their own jobs.

*Cassette users can have students listen to the script on the tape.

B. Read this.
The teacher can read this story to the class, check for comprehension of vocabulary and then students can read to themselves or to partners. Students turn their books over to read the answer.

C. Interview your partner.
1. Act out example. "Have you ever…?" "Yes. First, I…" Explain that students will write their partners' experiences.

2. Circulate to provide help if needed. Then have volunteers read their partner's stories to the class.

Unit Fifteen Evaluation

Page 201 🔲 ***I. Listening Comprehension****

      1. Go over the directions for Part I with students.

      2. Read each item of the script two times, at normal conversational speed.

          Script:

          1. I want to work full time.

          2. I have four years' experience.

          3. I'm calling about the job opening I saw in the newspaper.

          4. She has to fill out an application form.

          5. I was a carpenter for five years.

          6. I'm calling about the job opening.

          7. Do you have any references?

          8. What's the name of the company?

      *Cassette users can have students listen to the script on the tape.

Page 202 ***II. Reading and III. Writing***

      1. Go over the directions for Parts II and III with students.

      2. Have class do these sections independently.

Evaluation Check

      1. Correct evaluation by having student volunteers write their answers on the board or an overhead transparency.

      2. Have class check their answers.

      3. Circulate to make sure students have checked their work accurately.

Lesson 46

Meeting Co-workers

Communication Objectives:
Present or accept an award
Talk about personal history
Make conversation at a social event

New Structures:
Present perfect (regular verbs)
Prepositions *for* and *since*

Visuals:
V127   They have hired caterers for the reception.
V128   They have hired a band to play music.
V129   They have ordered a flower arrangement.
V130   They have ordered a cake.
V131   They have planned a special program.
V132   Let's Talk: I Have Wanted This Award for a Long Time

Other instructional aids: A prize for the Tic Tac Toe winner
An 8½" x 11" paper for each student

Page 204

✔ Review: Have You Ever Been...?

1. Ask students to write as many names of occupations on the chalkboard as they can.

2. Give each student a paper and guide them as they fold it into thirds in each direction to form a nine part Tic Tac Toe grid.

3. Have students select nine occupations and write one in each square.

4. Instruct them to circulate around the room and ask each other, "Have you ever been a/an (occupation)?" When they get a *yes* answer, they ask that student to sign the square.

5. Three in a row, and they win. You can award a prize if you wish.

Something New: Employee Recognition Day

1. Explain lesson objective: To make work–related small talk.

2. Show V127 and identify the caterers. Model the sentence. Repeat this procedure for each of the visuals.

3. Ask *yes/no* and *either/or* questions about the visuals. Students will answer "Yes, they have" or "No, they haven't."

4. Ask and have class, groups, individuals give the sentences.

Page 205 ☛ **Practice: "When did they start?"**

Have class open their books and read the Something New and Practice sections in pairs. (Note: the use of Present Perfect in this context indicates an unspecified time in the past.)

Page 206 **Let's Talk:** I Have Wanted This Award for a Long Time*

1. Show the visual to establish the context of the conversation: The reception. An employee is getting an award. Ask students if they know anyone who has received an award for their performance at work.

2. Model the dialogue as students listen, indicating the speakers by pointing to the visual or other means.

3. Model the dialogue again.

4. Model the dialogue and have class repeat.

5. Take one role and have class take other role; then change roles.

6. Divide class in half and have each half take a role; then change roles.

7. Have volunteers say the dialogue for the class.

 8. Have class open books and practice the dialogue in pairs.

*Cassette users can have students listen to the dialogue first with books closed.

Page 207 ☛ **Practice: "How long have you worked here?"**

Students will practice small talk as though they were at the reception. Have them look at the illustrations and go over the conversations. Practice as a class, in groups, and pairs.

★ Something Extra: How Long Have You Been Unemployed?

1. Have students look at the illustration to establish the context of the conversation: As the couple leaves the reception, they see a panhandler who seems homeless.

2. Follow the procedure given in the preceding Let's Talk section for presenting the dialogue.

3. Have students practice in pairs.

4. If students want to, you might discuss students' thoughts on this scenario. They may want to contribute ideas about how the company or community could help or express their own views.

☛ Practice: "How long have you been here?"

1. Back at the reception, people are talking about how long they have been doing this or that.

2. Go over the illustrations and conversations.

3. Practice as a class and in pairs.

Reading: A Time Line*

1. Explain the time line in the student book by drawing one on the chalkboard. Discuss.

2. Have students look at the time line in the book and read independently or as a class.

3. Check with comprehension questions.

4. Ask "How long" questions that require *for* and *since*.

*Cassette users can have students listen to the Reading first with books closed.

✍ Writing

1. Go over directions with students.

2. Have students complete the sentences on their own.

3. Check answers by circulating around classroom. When students have completed this segment, they can write Manolo's story using *for* and *since*.

4. Invite volunteers to read their stories to the class. Listen for correct use of *for* and *since,* and model corrections if necessary.

A. Interview four people in your group.

 1. Form groups of four or more students. Go over directions with class.

2. Act out asking someone the question, receiving the answer, and then writing down the answer. Instruct students to write answers for the members of their group.

3. Volunteers can share some of their answers with the class.

B. Draw a time line.

Review what a time line does. Go over the directions with the class. Encourage them to work in pencil as changes might need to be made. Before they start, discuss what important events might be included in their time lines.

C. Write your story.

Show students how to write a story from your own or a volunteer's time line. Then let students write on their own. Either have them read their stories to each other in groups, or check their writing by circulating around the class.

Lesson 47

Fixing Up A New House

Communication Objectives:

Discuss home improvement

Talk about finished and unfinished tasks

New Structures:

Present perfect (irregular verbs)

Adverbs *already* and *yet*

Visuals:

V133   Ted and Connie Duran's house, Phil and Miko Tanaka's house

V134   They've already painted the living room and kitchen.

V135   They haven't painted the bedrooms or bathrooms yet.

V136   Let's Talk: I Have Already Dug the Hole for the Tree

Other instructional aids:

Paper which can be torn into pieces, making a ticket for everyone in class to participate in a drawing

A basket to put the tickets in

A gift or two for the winner(s)

A pair of scissors

Page 212

✔ Review: How Long?

Have students make small talk by using the example questions as they move around the room and greet several students.

Something New: They've Lived There for Two Months

1. Explain lesson objective: Students will talk about fixing up a new house and about the tasks they have and haven't finished.

2. Show V133 and model the captions.

3. Ask "How long" questions about the Durans and the Tanakas to review *for* and *since*.

4. Show V134 and V135 and model the captions.

5. Ask students "Have they painted the bedroom yet?" and similar questions.

6. Ask more questions about the garage, the yard, etc. for practice.

☛ **Practice: "Have they planted the front yard?"**

Have students open their books and read what they have been practicing in the Something New and Practice sections.

Something New: They've Met Some New Neighbors

1. Point out that *worked, called, lived, painted,* etc. look like regular past verbs, which indeed they are, but that irregular verbs have an irregular form in the Present Perfect.

2. Have students look at the illustrations in the book and read the Something New sentences with you. Point out the irregular verbs *seen, bought, eaten, written, met,* and *gone.* List them on the board if you wish.

3. Ask *yes/no* questions about the sentences. Have students practice saying the whole sentence after giving the short answer. Ask *Wh–* questions about the pictures, such as "What kind of trees have they bought so far?"

4. Have pairs write 2–3 questions with "Have you" and irregular verbs they have learned.

5. Have volunteers ask you and/or other students their questions.

📼 **Let's Talk:** I Have Already Dug the Hole for the Tree*

1. Show the visual to establish the context of the conversation: The Tanakas are in their backyard. It's probably Saturday or Sunday. They're making plans.

2. Model the dialogue as students listen, indicating the speakers by pointing to the visual or other means.

3. Model the dialogue again.

4. Model the dialogue and have class repeat.

5. Take one role and have class take other role; then change roles.

6. Divide class in half and have each half take a role; then change roles.

7. Have volunteers say the dialogue for the class.

 8. Have class open books and practice the dialogue in pairs.

*Cassette users can have students listen to the dialogue first with books closed.

☛ Practice: "I've already made the bed"

1. Students will practice things they have already done in the past. Explain by acting out something you've already done: e.g., finished lunch or made the bed as in the first conversation.

2. Go over the illustrations and have students practice as a class and in pairs.

 3. Have class open books to Practice exercises.

Page 216 🖭 **Reading:** They Haven't Finished Yet*

1. Orient students, telling them they will read about the Tanakas and the Durans.

2. Have whole class or individuals read aloud or silently.

3. Ask comprehension questions.

4. Have students read the story again.

5. Ask students what they think the Tanakas should do.

*Cassette users can have students listen to the Reading first with books closed.

Page 217 ✍ **Writing**

1. Students might have said in the Reading segment that the Tanakas should invite their parents to visit. Tell them they are going to help the Tanakas write the letter.

2. Go over the directions with the students.

3. Read what is given of the letter. Tell students to refer back to the Reading if they can't remember what to write.

4. Ask volunteers to read their letters to the class.

Lesson 47 Activity Pages

Page 218 **A. Fill in the blanks with C for Carmen and L for Lito.**

1. Go over the directions with students.

2. Play the tape or read the script as many times as necessary.

3. Check orally, having class give answers.

Script:

Carmen: (Sleepily) Good morning.

Lito: Good morning. Have you gotten the paint brushes out?

Carmen: No, I haven't.

Lito: Have you washed the walls?

Carmen: No, I haven't.

Lito: Have you gotten the paint ready?

Carmen: No I haven't...Have you told me where the paint brushes are?

Lito: No, I haven't.

Carmen: Have you made the soapy water for the walls?

Lito: No, I haven't.

Carmen: Have you scraped the walls?

Lito: No, I haven't.

Carmen: Well, what have you been doing?

Lito: I've been thinking about all the work we have to do.

Carmen: Me, too.

Lito: I'm exhausted.

Carmen: Me, too.

Lito: Want to take a nap?

Carmen: Sure.

*Cassette users can have students listen to the script on the tape.

B. Read.

1. Let class discuss illustration.

2. Read to the class or have students read individually. Help students start writing by offering examples from your experience. Have volunteers share answers with class if you wish.

3. Circulate to check students' writing.

Page 219   ### C. Find someone in class who has done the things below.

Go over grid with students explaining that it's tic tac toe. If there is anyone who doesn't know this game, you might want to demonstrate the simple version with x's and o's. Go over directions. Remind students that only one person can sign a page. Practice questions students will ask each other. This is another activity where you can time students and award prizes for extra excitement.

Lesson 48

In the Neighborhood?

Communication Objectives:
Talk about recent activities
Talk about things you haven't done in a long time

New Structures:
Present perfect progressive

Visuals:
V137 The Allens have been watching TV
V138 Jim Forester has been washing his car
V139 Layne Drebin has been cooking
V140 The Galloway children have been skateboarding
V141 Let's Talk: I Have Been Waiting for You for an Hour

Page 220

✔ Review: I Have and I Haven't

1. In pairs have students tell each other about things they want to do to their homes. They can talk in terms of things they have and haven't done. Give examples about your home.

2. Have partners make lists, taking a piece of paper and folding it in half. One half is headed "Has," the other is "Hasn't." Partners should list what their partners tell them.

3. Volunteers should tell about their partners (referring to their lists). Show them how to say (name of partner) wants to (activity), but he/she hasn't done it yet.

Something New: What Have They Been Doing?

1. Explain lesson objective: To talk about things people have been doing. Show four visuals of people doing things. Tell students to imagine it's Saturday or Sunday morning in the neighborhood. Class will talk about what people have been doing all morning or all afternoon.

2. Identify the four activities. Model the captions for each visual.

3. Ask *yes/no* and *either/or* questions about the visuals.

4. Model and have class, groups, individuals repeat.

5. Ask and have class, groups, individuals answer to identify visuals.

Page 221 ☛ **Practice: "Since I was 10"**

1. Talk about yourself. Have a volunteer or you demonstrate a conversation in which you are asked how long you have been driving or how long you have been teaching.

 2. Have class open books read the Something New and Practice sections.

Page 222 🔲 **Let's Talk:** I Have Been Waiting for You for an Hour*

1. Show the visual to establish the context of the conversation: The Floreses are going to a housewarming party. They are getting ready to go. (Explain housewarming.)

2. Model the dialogue as students listen, indicating the speakers by pointing to the visual or other means.

3. Model the dialogue again.

4. Model the dialogue and have class repeat.

5. Take one role and have class take other role; then change roles.

6. Divide class in half and have them take the two roles; then have them switch roles.

7. Have volunteers say the dialogue for the class.

 8. Have class open books and practice the dialogue in pairs.

*Cassette users can have students listen to the dialogue first with books closed.

☛ **Practice: "Have you been waiting long?"**

1. Have class practice the question, "How long have you been waiting?"

 2. Have students open their books and practice in groups and pairs.

Page 223 ★ **Something Extra:** Since You Went Away...

1. Have students look at the illustration to establish the context of the conversation: The housewarming party.

2. Follow the procedure given in the Let's Talk section above for presenting the dialogue.

3. Have the students practice in pairs.

☛ Practice: "I haven't seen her in a long time"

1. Talk about some thing(s) you haven't done since you moved away from...: e.g., "I haven't...since I moved away..." Etc.

2. Ask students about things they haven't done since they left home. Prompt with "I haven't ... since I left my country." Encourage others to participate.

3. Have whole class practice, "I haven't...since I..."

 4. Have students open their books and practice the conversations in pairs.

Page 224 📼 **Reading and Writing:** Phil and Mike's Housewarming*

1. Go over directions for Part 1.

2. Have students read the conversation on their own and then write answers about themselves.

3. Have volunteers share their writing with the whole class.

4. Go over directions for Part 2.

5. Have pairs ask about each other, and then write answers about their partners.

6. Go over the directions for Part 3. Explain that they will write their sentences twice, once using *for* and once using *since*.

7. Ask a few students to answer the questions.

*Cassette users can have students listen to the Reading first with books closed.

Page 226

A. Complete these conversations with any language you want to use.

Go over the directions. Assign students to work in pairs. They can write anything they think someone would say—complete sentences or not—but model, "I've been..." as your answer for #1, S2. Have students practice the conversations they've written.

B. Interview three classmates and write their answers on the chart.

Go over directions. Review vocabulary. Have students circulate to fill in the chart. For someone who has not done #2 or #3, have them put a dash in the box.

Unit Sixteen Evaluation

Page 227 **I. Listening Comprehension***

    1. Go over the directions for Part I with students.

    2. Read each item of the script two times, at normal conversational speed.

> **Script:**
> 1. I have worked here for five years.
>
> 2. They hired caterers.
>
> 3. I have wanted this award for a long time.
>
> 4. They've already painted.
>
> 5. I have been unemployed for two years.
>
> 6. They have cleaned out the garage.
>
> 7. They have met some new neighbors.
>
> 8. The Allens have been watching TV all morning.

    *Cassette users can have students listen to the script on the tape.

Page 224 **II. Reading and III. Writing**

    1. Go over directions for Parts II and III with students.

    2. Have class do these sections independently.

Evaluation Check

    1. Correct evaluation by having student volunteers write their answers on the board or an overhead transparency.

    2. Have class check their answers.

    3. Circulate to make sure students have checked their work accurately.

Notes

Notes

Notes

Notes

Notes

Delta's Apple Pie, Teacher's Guide 2B

Notes

Notes